Praise for

Grow Up!

"Dr. Everett Piper's book *Not a Day Care* had the impact of a neutron bomb. In his groundbreaking sequel, *Grow Up!*, Dr. Piper continues the prophetic message that all need to hear but few have had the courage to say. Thank God someone tells the truth without apology!"
—**Mike Huckabee,** former governor of Arkansas

"If you want to slap today's current insanity in the face, read Dr. Everett Piper's new book, *Grow Up!* No one does a better job of identifying, addressing, and correcting the problems we confront with truth and wisdom."
—**Kevin D. Freeman,** host of *Economic War Room with Kevin Freeman* on BlazeTV

"Dr. Everett Piper thinks with clarity and speaks with forcefulness, a welcome relief from much of contemporary 'evangelicalism.' If you want to be coddled, don't read this. But if your heart hungers for truth from a modern-day Jeremiah, keep reading."
—**Dr. Jim Garlow,** CEO of Well Versed

"Dr. Piper is one of those under-the-radar thinkers who deserves more attention. His latest book, *Grow Up!*, should catapult him to the higher ranks of thoughtful people whose faith in the virtues and beliefs of our founders can endure if we will renew them."
—**Cal Thomas,** syndicated columnist

"Dr. Piper understands that a nation of children will cower in fear, while only adults have the courage to fight for freedom. *Grow Up!* is a book that everyone must read."
—**Trevor Shakiba,** president of Shakiba Capital

"Dr. Piper's wit and wisdom are once again on full display, as evidenced by his advice and admonition for younger generations to grow up rather than wake up—because 'wokeness' is an obstacle on the path toward personal accountability."
—**Bob Frantz,** Salem Media radio host

"Our culture is in desperate need of a clarion call to adult common sense. Dr. Everett Piper is that voice of reason and clarity. He's the adult in the room calling out the childishness and foolishness of the 'woke' crowd that expects to be coddled."
—**Patty David,** contributor to The Wesleyan Resistance

"Powerful, prophetic, and immensely clarifying! If your head is spinning as a result of the chaos our culture is drowning in, read this book. Dr. Piper's pen cuts through the chaos and brings hope for the future."
—**Jeff Keaton,** president and CEO of Renewanation

"Everett Piper's *Not a Day Care* diagnosed the root cause of our social ills: immaturity. More and more Americans just don't want adult responsibilities. Now with *Grow Up!*, Piper prescribes the cure to the problems plaguing our country. Young Americans who want to lead happy and fulfilled lives should make it a national bestseller."
—**Dennis Prager,** nationally syndicated radio talk show host and bestselling author of *The Rational Bible*

"If there was ever a time that we needed to stop acting like a nation of spoiled adolescents and *grow up*, it's now. Piper says it best—life isn't safe, but it's certainly worth living to the fullest."
—**Sam Sorbo,** actress, radio host, and author

Grow Up!

Grow Up!

Life Isn't Safe, but It's Good

Dr. Everett Piper

National Bestselling Author of *Not a Day Care*

with Jake McCandless and Andy Clapp

REGNERY
PUBLISHING
A Division of Salem Media Group
Washington, D.C.

Regnery® is a registered trademark of Salem Communications Holding Corporation

ISBN: 978-1-68451-091-7
eISBN: 978-1-68451-117-4

Library of Congress Control Number: 2020952233

Published in the United States by
Regnery Publishing
A Division of Salem Media Group
Washington, D.C.
www.Regnery.com

Manufactured in the United States of America

10 9 8 7 6 5 4 3 2 1

Books are available in quantity for promotional or premium use. For information on discounts and terms, please visit our website: www.Regnery.com.

To my grandchildren,

Though I know you not yet, may these words ring true as you "move beyond the elementary teachings . . . and be taken forward to maturity."

Much love,

Grandpa (with kudos to Saint Paul)

CONTENTS

A Time Such as This

I t's "1984," and we are living in schizophrenic times.
Dickensian times. Orwellian times. The best of times, but yet the worst. Times where we demand the truth while reveling in our lies. Times of great material gain but of even greater moral loss. Times of calling good evil and evil good; bitter sweet and sweet bitter. Times of the "tolerant" not tolerating what they find intolerable.

For all of our technological advancement, we have witnessed shocking mental decline. Silicon Valley magnate Mark Zuckerberg says Facebook honors our Constitution's commitment to free speech and equality, but his company's staff censors paragraphs of the Declaration of Independence because they find it to be antithetical to diversity and inclusion. California legislators, who claim to be proponents of truth and "fairness for all," propose legislation that would make it unlawful, even for those within the church, to provide products or services that specifically help congregants learn how to govern their behavior within the boundaries of what the Bible says is fair, right, moral, and true.

These are times when the Colorado Civil Rights Commission denies an artist the civil right to paint, craft, and bake images consistent with his moral convictions and to produce art that accurately reflects his worldview and his passions.

These are times when colleges and universities in nearly every state of the union are issuing speech codes that require faculty and students to stop honoring the millennia-old practice of using gender-specific pronouns and, instead, immediately adopt the tortured grammatical nonsense of ze, zer, zim, and zis. We've seen this happen at storied institutions such as UC Berkeley, the purported "birthplace of free speech."

These are times when Jews such as Dennis Prager, David Horowitz, and Ben Shapiro are protested, shunned, and banned by those who claim to stand against ghettos, gulags, and racism. Times when Candace Owens, a black woman, is heckled out of a restaurant by a bunch of white students chanting, "Down with white supremacy."

These are times when those who claim to champion democracy will boycott a restaurateur who dares to participate in the democratic process. These same cultural elites no longer even attempt to hide their disdain for the self-evident truths upon which our country and our culture was founded. Freedom of speech, freedom of religion, freedom of association, freedom of expression, and freedom in general are now considered antiquated and inferior ideas that should be discarded and replaced by the capricious whims of a governing class that believes the unwashed masses are too foolish to manage their own freedom.

They promote intolerance under the banner of "tolerance" and fascism under the flag of "freedom."

From our schools, where open debate and proper grammar are now prohibited, to our places of work, where ordinary Americans can be put out of business for advocating the wrong causes in their private life, no place is safe from the vindictive rage of the cultural elites.

Freedom means slavish adhesion to their dictates, and anyone who disagrees with their contrived notions of progress can be treated in the most barbarous fashion.

It is shameless duplicity.

It is self-refuting hypocrisy.

It is literal nonsense on parade.

Any schoolboy can see that the left does not care about tolerance. Tolerance, as the other slogans the left claims to champion, is window dressing for a brutal form of dominance that accepts no dissent. These self-styled advocates of "freedom and peace" are only interested in tyranny and power.

We see them on our campuses, in our courts, in our culture, and even in our churches, with their angry red faces of "love" shouting, "You must believe everything we believe!" No dissent, no differences, and no diversity. It is the rule of the gang—a worldview of unquestioned and unchallenged power. Their bumper sticker is "Conquest," not "Coexist." They are interested only in lockstep compliance, not reasonable compromise.

To paraphrase Martin Niemöller: "First they came for the bakers and I said nothing because I wasn't a baker. Then they came for the photographer and I said nothing because I wasn't a photographer. Then they came for the florists and I said nothing because I wasn't a florist. Then they came for the conservative black woman and the conservative Jew and I said nothing because I wasn't black or Jewish. When they came for me, there was no one left to speak."

So to repeat: these are trying times, difficult times, maybe even end-times.

An end to manners, politeness, courtesy, dignity, and mutual respect. An end to tolerance under the banner of "tolerance." An end to feminism under the banner of "MeToo." An end to women's rights under the banner of "trans-women's rights." An end to children's rights under the banner of "the right to abort children." An end to adults under the banner of "adulting."

We find ourselves in a country that has lost its way, a country in which an infantilized culture of tweets and tantrums dominates the public sphere. We are immersed in a culture of yelling rather than listening, a society of demands rather than dignity. We live in a time of perpetual adolescence and grown-up children, not one of mature adults who have truly grown up.

●   ●   ●

The week before Thanksgiving in 2015, a harsh experience woke me up to the convoluted times we inhabit. I was the president of Oklahoma Wesleyan University, a Christian college that still required chapel service twice a week for all students and faculty. That morning, I received a phone call from my dean of students.

"Dr. Piper, I just want to give you a heads-up," he began. "I was the speaker in chapel today. After I finished my talk, one of our students approached me at the podium. He pointed his finger in my chest and said, 'You offended me by singling me and my peers out. You made us feel uncomfortable.'"

"What was the topic of your talk?" I asked. "What did you say that offended him so badly?"

The dean's response was simple and brief. "1 Corinthians 13," he said—the paradigmatic discussion of love in the Bible. I would have thought the Pauline text stood among the least offensive passages in all of scripture. It's one that scores of Christians have read at their weddings.

I asked the dean for a copy of his sermon notes. I wanted to read them to see if there was any logical explanation for our student's indignation. Perhaps there was some political humor or some sort of misunderstood sarcasm that missed the mark. Much to my surprise, I found absolutely nothing in the sermon that could be deemed offensive. There was no sarcasm, nor was there any political message. His chapel talk was nothing but a brief homily on love—what Saint Paul called the greatest of all virtues.

I was stunned. One of my faculty had preached on the importance of sacrificial and self-giving love, and in response a student complained because he felt victimized. The student was outraged by the sermon's moral content. According to him, he had been made to feel uncomfortable for not showing love. In his mind, the speaker was wrong for making him and his peers feel guilty for falling short of the mark. Someone had challenged him about his shortcomings, which apparently was not allowed. In response, that person had to be a "hater," a "bigot," an "oppressor," and a "victimizer." The snowflake revolution had come to my campus.

For well over a decade, I had been writing opinion pieces for our local small-town newspaper. Because this nearly inexplicable student reaction was heavy on my mind, I decided to make the interaction the topic of my weekly column. I treated my article as a chance to pen an open letter to my students, their parents, this young man, and his peers, and anyone else who cared to listen.

Here is part of what I said:

> *Young man, that feeling of discomfort you have after listening to a sermon is called your conscience. An altar call is supposed to make you feel bad. It is supposed to make you feel guilty. The goal of many a good sermon is to get you to confess your sins—not coddle you in your selfishness. The primary objective of the Church and the Christian faith is your confession, not your self-actualization.*
>
> *Let me offer some advice:*
>
> *If you want the chaplain to tell you you're a victim rather than tell you that you need virtue, this may not be the university you're looking for. If you want to complain about a sermon that makes you feel less than loving for not showing love, this might be the wrong place.*
>
> *If you're more interested in playing the "hater" card than you are in confessing your own hate; if you want to arrogantly lecture, rather than humbly learn; if you don't want to feel guilt in your soul when you are guilty of sin; if you want to be enabled rather than confronted, there are many universities across the land that will give you exactly what you want, but this isn't one of them.*
>
> *At this university, we will teach you to be selfless rather than self-centered. We are more interested in you practicing*

personal forgiveness than political revenge. We want you to model interpersonal reconciliation rather than foment personal conflict. We believe the content of your character is more important than the color of your skin. We don't believe that you have been victimized every time you feel guilty and we don't issue "trigger warnings" before altar calls.

This university is not a "safe place," but rather, a place to learn: to learn that life isn't about you, but about others; that the bad feeling you have while listening to a sermon is called guilt; that the way to address it is to repent of everything that's wrong with you rather than blame others for everything that's wrong with them. This is a place where you will quickly learn that you need to grow up.

This is not a day care. This is a university.

Now, I generally assume that only five people read my small-town paper opinion columns, and that of those, only three care. But this week was different. I don't know the secrets of what makes something "go viral," but before I knew it over 3.5 million people had clicked on this story. Members of the American press corps, from major cable news outlets to political journals and publications, all ran stories on my little opinion piece, and newspapers and magazines in Great Britain and Asia were all interested. NBC's *Today* even cited the brouhaha my column caused as one of the top ten news stories of the year for 2015!

Apparently, I had said something many were waiting to hear. My simple and brief response struck a chord. Many who openly disagreed with what they called "my religion and my politics" wrote, texted, emailed, or called me to thank me for expressing a rebuke of an entitled generation of students. The overwhelming majority of responses to my column—97 percent, by my count—were positive. I had written something that struck a nerve.

Millions of Americans chimed in to affirm what I said because they knew something is desperately wrong in our society. They know that the bad behavior they see reported on the nightly news has to have a cause, and that the juvenile tantrums they are watching at our country's most storied institutions did not just spring out of thin air. They intuitively understand that the immaturity, self-absorption, and pervasive narcissism that defines college students is no longer restricted to college campuses, but now pervades our culture at large. Bad behavior doesn't just spring from a vacuum: it has a cause.

A Threatening Mess

"Not a Day Care" resonated with so many readers because all of us know in our heart of hearts that civilizations stand and fall by the power of ideas. Military conquest may capture the imaginations of our historians, but the paths of empires and nations are determined by the convictions their people hold. Americans know that the slogans protestors chant are inauspicious signs of their country's future. And childish pouts of "me and mine" can almost always be traced back to one key source.

Bad teaching tends to create a distorted understanding of how the world works and one's role within it. Today, bad teaching has led large swathes of society to throw collective temper tantrums. What we teach in our schools is now bearing itself out in the behavior we see in our streets. As Abraham Lincoln is reported to have said, "The philosophy of the schoolroom in one generation will become the philosophy of the government in the next." Even Hitler understood this simple truth when he said, "Let me control the schools, and I will control the state." What is taught in a nation's classrooms will be practiced in that nation's boardrooms, courtrooms, and living rooms.

Selfishness as well as sacrifice always has a cause, and that cause, in great measure, can nearly always be traced back to what we teach our children. Solomon was simple and clear: "Train up a child in the way he should go and when he is old, he will not depart." There is great power in ideas, and that power can be wielded for either noble or nefarious ends.

Richard Weaver drove home this point in 1948 when he wrote his seminal work *Ideas Have Consequences*. Weaver's thesis was simple, so simple that you hardly have to read beyond the cover to understand his message. Weaver dared to believe that ideas matter. They always bear fruit. There is no such thing as a neutral idea, and all ideas are directional. Those fruits that ideas produce can be seen in our communal life. Good ideas bear good culture, good government, good community, good church, and good kids, whereas bad ideas bear the opposite. If you want to live in a society that has those good things rather than their opposites, you need to make sure that your society is permeated with good ideas.

The fact that Weaver wrote his influential book in 1948 is no accident. When Weaver looked back at the world at war just a few years earlier, he saw that the evil the world suffered at the hands of the Third Reich, Mussolini, Stalin, and the Empire of the Rising Sun was as predictable as the sunrise. Given the ideas which those regimes committed themselves to and promulgated among their citizenry, the atrocities of National Socialism, the Ukrainian famine, and the Nazi Holocaust should have been no surprise. It's like your grandmother said: "Garbage in, and garbage out."

A Realistic Solution

In my book *Not a Day Care: The Devastating Consequences of Abandoning Truth*, I pointed out these problems. I sounded the alarm that education today is in crisis. I gave example after example of how the contemporary academy is no longer in the business of pursuing truth but rather is more interested in celebrating tolerance. I warned of the rising ideological fascism that now stands on the grave of education's proud tradition of academic freedom. I shared story after story of how today's schools, colleges, and universities look more like George Orwell's Ministry of Truth than they do institutions that actually believe they should be in the business of challenging propaganda rather than protecting it. I bemoaned the academy's worship of feelings over facts. I gave example after example of how pedantic elites, otherwise known as university professors, tell those with whom they disagree that they can't tolerate those they find intolerable and that they hate hateful people.

This is my industry, and I have to listen to this almost every day. Smart people actually say this stuff. It is literal nonsense, for it makes no sense. It's self-refuting at every turn. With their every word they saw away at the very branch upon which they sit. Their circular arguments smack of watching a dog chase its tail. It would be funny if it weren't so sad. They should know better. But they have been drinking their own Kool-Aid for so long they have come to believe their own lies.

M. Scott Peck warned of this. He called it the "diabolical human mind." Dr. Graham Walker did likewise when he wrote of "The Pathology of the Intellect." The apostle Paul calls it the reprobate mind. The message is the same from all three, along with Weaver: the longer we lie to ourselves, the more prone we become to believing our own lies. The more we believe our own deception, the less reason we have to change. There is no need to mature, to grow up, to act like an adult rather than a spoiled child or a self-absorbed adolescent, if we are comfortable in our own delusion. Ideas have consequences.

But there is an answer, and that is the purpose of this book. The answer is found in mature thinking and mature ideas. It is found in the old time-tested truths of the liberating arts. It is found in pursuing truth rather than protecting opinions. It is found in facts rather than feelings. It is found in the moral and intellectual laws that have been tested by time, defended by reason, validated by reason, and endowed to us by our Creator.

At its core, this book is meant to be a book of solutions. It offers good ideas versus bad, ideas of freedom versus fascism, ideas of self-giving versus selfishness. The pages that follow will not be those that bemoan the problem. We have done enough of that. This is a book about personal responsibility, not personal grievance. It is a book about virtue, not victims. This is a book about growing up rather than griping and grousing. This is a book of ideas, enduring ideas, ideas that have been proven by the test of time to work, ideas that actually help make us a mature nation of self-giving adults rather than a fragmented culture of self-centered children. This is a book about acting like an adult in an increasingly infantilized world.

Walking Is Better Than Crawling

"It's what you learn after you know it all that counts."

—Harry S. Truman

Cry Out Loud

We all come out of our mothers' wombs with a lot to learn. None of us knew how to walk from the day we were born. We started by crawling on the floor; then we slowly started moving with someone's help; and, at some point, we fearlessly stepped into the unknown. We took our first steps. Today, though we've likely never reflected on that moment, we're certainly thankful for the fact that we walked.

When we took those first steps, we took our first steps towards becoming fully functioning human beings. We grew and matured, and if we could have shared our toddler moments with our friends on social media at the time, we would have proudly boasted of our accomplishments. If we were able to scroll through all the proverbial posts of #toddlering, we'd notice that regardless of how that first step was shared, it would be considered an improvement, progression, maturation, or a graduation. That step would be recognized as a positive development.

Our friends and family would cheer and celebrate in response. They might LOL—laugh out loud—but in a way that expressed their support. They would be proud to see us on our way to becoming a healthy toddler.

Our first step was a milestone in our development, and everyone loves celebrating the accomplishments of people they love.

Our first steps would be followed by many other milestones that we and our family members take the time to celebrate. If we were to put them on social media, we'd share #firstwords, #talkingnow, #realunderwear, #toothfairy, #firstdayofschool, #icanreadnow, #homerun, #prom, #graduation, and many others. We celebrate and recognize these accomplishments as good, part and parcel of flourishing as a human being. We look forward to them and fill baby albums with them. In our culture, we still view these milestones as important and positive. We still value them. But when we reach the goal towards which all previous childhood, teenage, and college milestones were building—adulthood—we suddenly forget how important these milestones are to our continued growth.

You won't find #toddlering trending on social media, but there are scores of posts tagged #adulting. Maybe you or your kids are even guilty of such posts. Even if you're not, you have to admit that it's a cute phrase that makes clever use of irony. #Adulting posts can range from the relatively harmless "Nobody asks me what my favorite dinosaur is anymore" to the more concerning "I'm 27 and my mom still makes my doctor's appointments, if she didn't I'd just not go and probably die from something I could've completely avoided." Some tweets celebrate the mundane features of real life in comparison to childhood dreams, while others showcase the complete dysfunction of young adults. The latter kind of statements make many of us recoil because of the irresponsibility and apparent perpetual childishness they represent.

Older generations like to ridicule millennials, or whatever today's youngest generation is being called, for seeking awards and trophies for showing up. The Participation Trophy generations think they should get medals for performing everyday chores and life functions—things that we all must do. But meanwhile, they hardly perform the basic tasks that are asked of them as adults, and in the rare instances when they do, they demand recognition.

Older folk who grew up in a different time are deeply disturbed by this trend. They see it as a symptom of the general decline that has occurred in our institutions, a symptom of a problem that is consuming current and future generations, plaguing our universities, and will eventually cripple our nation.

It is alarming to many because they have lived long enough to see the value of the trials and travails of a life well-lived. They know from whence they speak. They have navigated these waters and they know where the rocks and the reefs are. They grew up in a time when the phrase "participation trophy" would have seemed oxymoronic. They went to work early in life, moved out of the house young, paid their own way, sacrificed, and, as Nike used to say, "just did it." These people embraced adulthood; they didn't hashtag it.

#Adulting isn't a laugh out loud for the future of America. For the lives of many young adults today and those they'll impact in the future it should be a cry out loud. It is a mirror in which we can see the misaligned views of our culture.

It's a Symptom

As a symptom, the reality behind the adulting jokes is malignant, and reveals a stage four societal cancer. This terminal disease isn't just the fault of the young, but a breakdown in our culture at large. Its genesis is ideological. It stems from political and social ideas that may have appeared right at one point, but which have proven themselves, through trial and error, to be clearly wrong—ideas that may have seemed novel and groundbreaking but which have proven to break little other than the very foundation upon which America, as well as most of the Western world, has been built. Richard Weaver warned of this over seventy years ago, writing "Ideas have consequences" in his book by the same name. His argument was simple. There is no such thing as a neutral idea. Value neutrality is a ruse. Ideas are always directional. Good ideas lead to good culture, good government, good corporations, and good communities.

Bad ideas lead to the opposite. For better and for worse, individuals, as well as countries and cultures, are shaped by their ideas. Ideas that are grounded in truth and reality can bring great good. And conversely, ideas that spring from lies and deception always cause great harm. Navigating these ideas and choosing which ones to claim as our own is the quest for adulthood—regardless of our age.

The often-trending "adulting" hashtag and the accompanying mindset provide damning evidence. The situation is dire for the young adults who find adulthood and its attendant responsibilities a laughing and begrudging matter. But the situation isn't just dire for those youths as individuals; it's also dire for the nation as a whole. As the younger generations grow into leadership positions, we as a people become more immersed in a culture of perpetual adolescents mired in a banal swamp of ideological despondency.

Beyond the tweets and selfies, real adulting has not yet come to pass for scores of American citizens. The *Washington Times* recently reported shocking data from the U.S. Census Bureau that illustrates the grim state of affairs: 35 percent of all eighteen- to thirty-four-year-old Americans live with their parents.[1] According to a study recently released by the Pew Research Center, 30 percent of millennial men between the ages of eighteen and thirty-three have no job, 10 percent higher than previous generations. Of that number, approximately 8 percent are unemployed, while 22 percent are not engaged in the workforce at all.[2] Reports across the country confirm that millennials are marrying less and later than any other generation in history. Four out of ten young adults in 2016 were recorded as being married, while in 1980 it was six out of ten.[3]

The picture does not look good for a cohort of young adults that boasts of being the most college-educated generation.[4] We could marshal dozens of studies to confirm what we all see with our own eyes: young Americans aren't engaging in responsible adult behavior that makes positive contributions to society.

Young adults shirk away from the mundane tasks that form the bedrock of a mature and developed life. They're moving out of suburban homes that need cleaning, maintenance, and love into cramped city condominiums where everything is taken care of for them. Instead of taking the time to prepare dinner and carry out household chores, they're ordering takeout and spending money on needless services. Millennials are so averse to domestic normalcy that many no longer use the top sheet on their bed.[5] Apparently they no longer see the obvious purpose and function of very simple things like sheets and bedding!

Without the supervision of their parents, millennials and the generations that follow them are prolonging their teenage years. They've clenched their fists and dug in their heels as they've been pushed to adulthood, resisting with every ounce of their being. While they've resisted the natural progression of life, choosing instead to arrest their own development, they've forced their absurd childish demands on the rest of society. The snowflake rebellion and the need for endless coddling are now playing out in every corner of American life. They don't just want to stew in their extended adolescence; they want to remake American government in their image. They advocate for an overbearing government with policies that bring more dependency, less personal responsibility, and, one could argue, more prolonged adolescence and immaturity.

But lest you think I am just blaming millennials and GenZers, let me be clear: blame also lies with their parents. Many of the ideas the boomers institutionalized and the personal decisions they made have set the stage for this dysfunction. Boomer parenting was the equivalent of surgically removing a student's frontal lobe before demanding that he explain an algebraic formula, or removing a girl's legs while asking her to run a race. The prolonged adolescence, social dysfunction, and psychological fragility of the millennials is the legacy of the baby boomers. The boomers have left their progeny these qualities as an inheritance. To put it in different terms, we boomers have given our kids a culture and a country where, as C.S. Lewis warned, we have "gelded the stallion and bid him be fruitful." We have removed our nation's character and expect its citizens to show courage. My generation has "created men without chests" and demands virtue of them.

This lunacy of creating a culture of perpetual dependency is what led to my first book, *Not a Day Care*. It's also what brings many in the younger generations to "feel the Bern" and fall in line with the likes of Bernie Sanders, AOC, and those who preach that socialism will cure all that ails us.

The differences between the snowflake generations and their predecessors are clear for all to see. The snowflakes whine and moan and turn to false prophets on the political left; the "Greatest Generation," that memorable group of Americans who built this country into a global superpower through hard work and sacrifice, gave everything they could to their country without expecting anything in return. No great civilization has ever made growing up and becoming an adult a joke or a hashtag. No successful culture has ever bemoaned adulthood as something to lament. And most importantly, no civilization has stretched out the start of adulthood as long as America is doing now and survived. We are in uncharted waters that will have ramifications for us all.

The English language has borrowed quite a few idiomatic phrases from watching ducks with their offspring. We've all seen the charming scene of a mother duck waddling to her destination with a long line of her babies in tow. Sometimes, when the mother manages to keep her babies in an orderly formation, we see that she has her "ducks in a row." But often, one of the baby ducklings will break formation—one duckling will be an "odd duck." An orderly line of ducklings makes it easy to tell which one might be eccentric. The orderly line makes it easier to mark the odd duck.

If we were to stretch young American adults from every generation out in a line, the twenty-something-year-old of the present would stand out as the odd duck. We would immediately recognize him, irrespective of the clothes or gadgets he had. Modern dress, haircuts, and Apple Watches would hardly be needed to distinguish our American youth from the American youth of times past. You see, the youths of earlier generations relished the idea and role of becoming adults.

The same would hold true if we lined up youths from great civilizations in the past. Again, our contemporary young friends would be a proverbial orange among apples. Just as the American youths of earlier days were eager for adulthood and its attendant responsibilities, so too were the young men and women of Rome, Egypt, and Mesopotamia. No matter what time or where you went around the world to find young adults, you would find that they viewed adulthood as superior to childhood. Only our young adults seem to disagree.

Throughout known history, growing up, progressing, and becoming a mature man or woman has been eagerly anticipated. Childhood and teenage years were meant to prepare young men and women for their years of maturity. And during those preparatory years there was a yearning to be a free, responsible, and mature human being—otherwise known as an adult. There were childhood dreams and teenage desires: move out of the house, get a job, make a living, build a career, accept responsibility, and make a contribution to one's society. No one aspired to barely provide for himself and pine after childhood, doing the equivalent of sitting in his apartment and eating Ramen noodles while binging on Netflix and Pokémon.

Sure, the economic depressions through which we've lived don't help. And as we've mentioned, the failed parenting techniques and cultural aspirations of the baby boomers certainly bear some responsibility. But I would argue that the contemporary mindset of perpetual adolescence is the product of bad education. The philosophical foolishness of the academy has trickled down, shaping and molding our world one graduating class at a time. These college graduates, educated to take leadership roles in society, think that it should be cared for while not having a clue about the priorities of mature life. They have been taught to think of the world in childish and imbecile ways; it should be no surprise that they leave their respective campuses as childish imbeciles.

How can we get out of this vicious cycle of dependency and selfish focus? How can we quit being the odd duck and fall in line? While it's a

Herculean task, we must find a way to learn from our predecessors and retrieve the common sense of past generations.

We Must Learn

Every society has a set of norms and expectations—you could call them rules or guidelines for the individuals that make up the community. Those norms and expectations are meant to teach people how to act. Being a functioning adult in a given place means adhering to those rules. The rules, which may be flawed, are general teachers of what it means to be a part of the group.

For a boy to become a man, or for a girl to become a woman, they had to grow in the ways prescribed to them. That growth took place through education, whether that meant the formal book learning of the schools or the informal education of experience. In fact, it could be argued the entire point of education is to learn and grow. Education turns unformed youths and adolescents into useful, productive members of society. Through education, a society teaches people to function, work, and keep useful knowledge alive by passing it down to following generations. That's why every society invests so many resources into teaching. From the point of view of the individual, learning how to act in society is the reason for learning. It's the reason schools were created in the first place. It's the reason for the ivory tower. Every college and university had a specific reason for its founding. This was called its mission! Whether it was Oxford, Cambridge, Harvard, Dartmouth, Princeton, or Yale, each school had a mission statement that made it quite clear why it was necessary and why it existed. Quite simply, every one of them was established to teach students how to think and act like intelligent, thoughtful, moral, and mature human beings.

We can go beyond formal education and consider learning itself. From the time we are a baby we begin learning. Every time we utilize our senses, we learn and grow and increase in our function. When we know more, we can do more. As infants learning about the world, we lay the building blocks that will act as the foundation for adulthood and the rest of our lives. We're setting the rungs of a ladder we'll climb into adulthood.

Education is always oriented toward certain milestones. Whether mastering a subject, learning concrete skills, or apprenticing in a trade, we're always moving toward a particular accomplishment that will be of general use to our community. Whether that's individual, like the example of learning to walk we discussed earlier, or some form of social recognition, like receiving a license or degree, we're always pushing forward toward an ability that we can share with our peers.

Historically, and in many cultures, there are rites of passage that form the centerpiece of one's life. These moments celebrate the move from adolescence to adulthood, or toward adulthood. Today, we're most familiar with the bar and bat mitzvahs of the Jews. The former celebrates a boy's transition to manhood, while the latter celebrates a girl's ascension to womanhood. But Jewish culture is certainly not the only one to express rites of passage. In Hispanic culture, people celebrate the quinceañera. Even the Amish Rumspringa is familiar in pop culture today.

Dozens of cultures celebrate rites of passage, and some of those rites are better known to the broader public than others. In cultures that have clear rites of passage, the transition into adulthood is viewed and respected and honored. While our American rites of passage may not be as symbolic, we certainly have unofficial milestones that serve a similar function. Arbitrary events like graduation, getting a first real job, turning a particular age, marriage, and having a child all act in a similar way to what other cultures express in ritual practice. Some argue, with some merit, that the lack of clearly defined rites of passage has caused confusion among our youth. Many of the events we consider as proxies for formal ceremonies are poorly defined and create uncertainty.

But even without that clarity of a ceremonial rite of passage, past generations in America looked at one's integrity and personal responsibility as a predicate to citizenship. Even further back, when most American families lived on farms and were nearly self-sufficient, becoming an adult was akin to "survival" or, to put it differently, actually "existing."

The current mindset that results in perpetual adolescence is promoted and propagated by pop culture, education, and the media. Encouraging perpetual adolescence is a profitable business, but in the long run we will all foot the bill. Instead of inculcating our next generations in a culture that discourages them from becoming adults, we need to educate them with a new message. We need to take the transition to adulthood seriously, which means that we need to take the time of preparation as a stepping-stone to something better, not the peak of life from which everything goes downhill.

Preparation implies practice. And practice often means studying, listening, and learning. And learning obviously means education. When it comes to becoming a mature person or a mature culture, education matters, whether formal or informal. Think of all you've learned in your life and how that has moved you forward—forward to being an adult. From opening our eyes, learning to eat, roll over, crawl, pull up, walk, eat solid foods, run, jump, skip, ride a bicycle, the alphabet, letter sounds, numbers, how to read, how to add, how to subtract—you get the picture. Education has moved you forward.

Not just learning, but learning new, hard things. Our minds, our bodies, and our wills have to be stretched. We don't grow by rehearsing what we have already mastered, but rather by being challenged.

We all know this when it comes to personal fitness. When working out with resistance training, we actually tear and break down our muscles. The process of breaking and rebuilding results in strength and endurance. We sculpt the body by imposing stress and pain on it.

Another example is that of making a snowman. To build Frosty, we don't need a corncob pipe, a button nose, and two eyes made out of coal. We don't even need a magic hat. What we need is the hard work of rolling, packing, and forming loose snow into big snowballs that are hoisted, pushed, and pulled on top of one another. Additionally, we all know that the best snowmen are those that have been exposed to some of the sun's heat. It is the melting process that fuses the various parts together into a cohesive whole.

The principle of "no pain, no gain," of being refined by fire, is antithetical to the driving ethos of the snowflake rebellion sweeping across our nation's campuses. It is a principle that seems completely lost in places like the colleges and universities that disinvite speakers, petition to get teachers fired, and work overtime to insulate students from ideas that challenge their worldview. The present generation of college students riots against speakers because the speakers have the audacity to challenge what the students already believe. They have the temerity to suggest that eighteen- to twenty-two-year-olds might actually be wrong.

In the name of openness these students are closed-minded. In the interest of tolerance they are intolerant. Under the banner of inclusion they exclude everyone who makes them uncomfortable. This is not a recipe for growth but rather one for stagnation. This is perpetual adolescence. This is not adulthood.

Remember: growth and maturity are unequivocally good. And, at the same time, growth and maturity require learning—not just learning, but learning from hard truths. No pain, no gain. Avoiding challenging ideas or experiences means no growth, no progression, and no maturation. Avoiding real education leaves you stuck in adolescence and prevents you from adulthood.

If we want an adult culture and not a nation full of a bunch of spoiled twenty-five-year-old teenagers, we should focus on the ideas that have been proven by the test of time. We should teach our children the best ideas that history shows work, rather than the avant-garde thinking that has been proven over and over again to fail.

There is a paradox in growing up, immortally expressed in the words of C.S. Lewis: "Once you were a child. Once you knew what inquiry was for. There was a time when you asked questions because you wanted answers, and were glad when you had found them. Become that child again. . . . Thirst was made for water; inquiry for truth."

Learning to walk always involves falling and failing. It also implies admitting you don't know everything and that it might be smart to pay attention to someone who's already done it. No one wants to be affirmed and tolerated for crawling his way through life. Whether it be intellectually, morally, or socially, walking is always better than crawling.

The apostle Paul makes a similar point in his letter to the Corinthians: "When I was a child, I spoke like a child, I thought like a child, I reasoned like a child. When I became a man, I gave up childish ways."

Plates Don't Have Legs

"Ask not what your country can do for you, ask what you can do for your country."

—President John F. Kennedy

A Failure to Teach, a Failure to Launch

"I can't do it. Can you do it for me?"

That's the demand of a child. His plea comes from a place of inability, not ability. Maybe it's a jar he cannot open. Perhaps it's something that's too high to reach on a shelf.

The difference between the life of a child and that of an adult is that, over time, kids are given more responsibility, taught how to do various tasks, and pushed to use their newfound skills to provide for themselves.

Those who are never given responsibility and who are not encouraged to do things for themselves never grow. They are stunted and live at a level of performance far below that of their peers. They seem to be frozen in time, recoiling from responsibility. They always look outward as they cast blame or shirk responsibility. Their constant default response to new challenges is to blame others for their difficulties, or to look towards someone else to do it for them.

That sentiment is the defining characteristic of our time. "It's not my job." "I can't do it." "Someone else can do it for me." It's called entitlement. At its core, it's simple laziness.

Often these demands are made in spite of individual ability. People can do the tasks at hand, they just don't want to. So they lie to themselves by saying, "I can't do it." And they lie to others by asking, "Can you do it for me?" The ability is there, but the desire is absent.

Needing help is a part of life, but expecting someone else to do what we can do for ourselves is another issue. And it's an issue plaguing our culture today. By acting as children who demand that others do things for us, we've destroyed the concept of personal responsibility and personal initiative in one generation and are in the process of destroying human dignity and human freedom in the next.

It seems that somewhere along the line we have forgotten the obvious fact that becoming an adult means accepting responsibility for our own actions. Rather than celebrating the freedom and independence that comes from the risk of doing things ourselves, we've embraced safety as our highest good by shamefully expecting others to do for us what we could do for ourselves. Why risk coming out of our "safe space" if someone else is always there to think for us, pay for us, and work for us? Might as well just stay put in Mom and Dad's basement as long as they do the laundry, cook the meals, and charge no rent. If safety is what life is all about, what could be better than that?

A friend once shared a story with me about a teenager he knew. The teen rarely came out of his room and spent most of his days playing video games. On his sixteenth birthday, his parents surprised him and bought him a car. On the morning of the big day, as he unwrapped a small package with the car keys in it, his parents expected him to rush out to get his license and explore a new world with his newfound freedom. But this kid did the exact opposite. Rather than driving himself in his brand new car, he still preferred that his parents chauffer him around to school, church, and other places he wanted to go. Rather than assume the risk that comes with responsibility and freedom, he was content to remain dependent and safe, never considering the load he was continuing to put on his parents. He had his own car, something a lot of teens would give their eyeteeth to have, but he was content to simply say, "I can't do it. Can you do it for me?"

Unfortunately, this story is hardly unique or uncommon. You're probably saying, "I know that kid" or "I have heard this one before." And it's not just a story about lazy sixteen-year-old boys. The attitude displayed by this particular boy is pervasive. It's a ubiquitous mark of the dysfunction in American culture and American life.

Rather than teaching responsibility and encouraging others to take charge of their own lives, we have preached security and safety at the expense of all other values. This has inevitably led to perpetual infantilization and its consequent laziness. One generation after another expects everybody else to do it for them rather than assuming the obligation of doing things for themselves.

The teenager mentioned above eventually went off to college. He did not drive his own car to campus, but was driven there by his parents. By the end of the first semester, which Mommy and Daddy paid for, he was back home. He flunked out because no one was there to hold his hand and force him to get up in the morning and go to class. Evidently, not only could he not drive a car, but he also did not know how to use the alarm clock function on his smartphone that he had glued to his hand every minute of every day—a phone that, again, his parents bought him. (Yes, shame on the parents.)

Being content with the comfort of childhood, this kid lacked any motivation to grow up. His perpetual adolescence jeopardized his future. The problem of a lack of initiative never corrected itself. The problem, in fact, had metastasized into a cancer that sucked the motivation out of what could have been a promising opportunity.

Any father or mother worth their salt knows that a number one rule of parenting is that giving your kids the most basic and elementary responsibilities gives them the opportunity to succeed in life. Requiring our kids to assume responsibility for even the most menial of tasks, like making their bed, cleaning their room, feeding the dog, and mowing the lawn, teaches that working is what adults do and taking is what children do. There is a thing called "taking initiative," and it's always better than taking money and expecting others to do it for us.

You don't have to be a child psychologist to figure out the likely script for this young friend's early life. First, there were the dirty plates and cups left on the dinner table that the parents picked up, carried to the sink, washed, dried, and put up. Then there was the filthy room and dirty laundry that Junior was never held accountable for. Next there was a car collecting dust in a driveway. Finally, we see a young man still acting like a spoiled little boy, living back in his room, with no job and stacks of Red Bull cans sitting around his gaming console. The nest was warm and safe. Why leave? If someone else is going to continue to provide free stuff and a carefree life, why learn how to fly?

Houston, we have a problem, and it's not regarding reentry. We have a failure to launch.

Exam Canceled

Right after the 2016 presidential election, a University of Michigan psychology professor postponed a required exam because he believed his students were too traumatized by the GOP victory. Apparently his students couldn't turn their night-lights off because they believed that the big bad Trump monster was going to come out from under their beds to eat them all up.

At the same time, Columbia University professors postponed exams for similar reasons, and one professor at the University of Connecticut allowed students to skip class without penalty.

Universities from Berkeley to Brown provided counseling centers complete with Play-Doh, coloring books, crayons, and videos of frolicking puppies to help soothe the anxieties of their precious darlings.

A university in New England brought in a small herd of goats so its students would have their own little petting zoo to calm their anxieties and fears during finals week.

Emory University's president issued a public apology to all of his students because someone had used sidewalk chalk to write the name

Trump on a campus walkway. Students reportedly felt triggered by this obvious microaggression.

It appears that in all these examples (and literally dozens more like them from coast to coast), both students and faculty considered their preferred candidate's loss to be a hand-in-glove precursor to their losing their own minds.

The lesson learned that day on all of these campuses of supposed higher learning was simple—if life doesn't give you the results you want, you don't have to work, you don't have to perform, you can neglect your responsibilities and blame it all on someone else. Go cuddle a puppy. Go pet a goat and someone else will do life for you.

Such a failure by those entrusted to teach and lead our students screams that the lie of the good life being one and the same as the comfortable and safe life is so pervasive in our present culture that it cannot be left unaddressed.

The problem has roots in the struggle for control. When we prize security over freedom, we give control to those who promise to protect and provide for us. And once we give such authority to someone else, we have no means by which to challenge their rule over our lives. Furthermore, if someone else does everything for us, we are robbed of a drive to do anything for ourselves. Laziness sets in. Stagnation and dependency become our default position. Freedom is lost. We are frozen in childhood dependency. We never grow up.

Breaking this vicious cycle of comfort, safety, and dependency has to be intentional and always requires hard work.

The obligation to take responsibility is a logical demand of becoming an adult. It has nothing to do with our feelings, our fears, or our likes and dislikes. It is a conscious act. It is the knowledge that we must do something even though we don't want to. It is the knowledge and acceptance that there is a right way to do something that might not always be pleasant. Another phrase for this process is called delayed gratification.

Relaxation at the end of a tough stretch is rewarding when it is the reward for our labor.

Being able to push through setbacks, trials, and struggles is a sign of growth. It is evidence of an individual's growing up and maturing.

Adulthood has little to do with age and everything to do with character. It is the result of training the inner man. It represents the heart and soul of who we truly are, both individually and collectively.

The more dependent we become on other human beings, the less independent we are in the totality of life. Those who promote a culture of avoiding responsibility understand that creating dependency means gaining control. All the despots of history have known this. Pol Pot, Mao, Stalin, Castro, and Mussolini all understood that people who take personal responsibility for their lives are people they could not control. They knew that the number one rule for stealing freedom is to get the masses to point the finger of responsibility outward rather than inward. As long as you can get the proletariat to blame the bourgeoisie, the tyrant will win. As long as you can get the 99 percent to accuse the 1 percent, you can kill freedom and gain power. Get women to blame men, or blacks to blame whites, or get green men to blame orange men—it doesn't matter. As long as the demagogue can get the masses to blame everyone but themselves he can crush liberty and gain control. It is the deadly combination of entitlement and enablement. The Roman emperors knew this, so they made sure to provide bread and circuses while they persecuted Christians.

This is why people show an inability to think for themselves today and why they wait to be told what to do. We are locked into perpetual adolescence because we know that when Mommy and Daddy stop providing for us, Uncle Sam will gladly step in.

Taking responsibility is fundamental to independence and growth. Those who are responsible choose their own path in life. They are free. Those who shirk responsibility are enslaved by those who are only too happy to take the responsibility for them. They become little more than lobotomized rodents—hypothalamus rats—who have no desire for independence, but are content to stay in their cage, safe and secure.

An expectation for others to do work that should be yours and to keep you safe and comfortable is, at its core, self-centered. It results in placing too much emphasis on what would make your world better rather than asking how you can make the world a better place for someone else.

It also results in being frozen in time as an incomplete and immature being.

It is a known fact that the struggle to fight its way out of the cocoon provides life-giving blood to the wings of the butterfly. If someone intervenes and breaks the cocoon open in an effort to "help" the butterfly, they leave it incomplete and incapable of flight.

In like manner, when we are spared the effort of working free from our "cocoon," we fail to emerge, grow, and mature. The fight is necessary for flight.

The alternative is to take away the very thing that produces the pumping blood of human dignity and human freedom. The more we coddle, the more bankrupt an entire generation becomes of the work ethic that is an essential trait of a free people and culture.

To avoid having a nation full of entitled and enabled thirty-year-old teenagers, it would be wise to revisit our obligation to teach our progeny the values of responsibility and freedom instead of safety and comfort.

Life Goes On

To fix a problem, we must see why the problem is a problem to begin with. We have to take a glance through the lens of tradition, reason, experience, and revelation to see why a pattern of thought leads to destructive behavior.

John F. Kennedy's quote about doing for the country rings as true today as it ever has. However, in the context of our current cultural conversation, a slight reframing of the statement might be pertinent.

Today, the statement could be, "Think not about what others can do for you, think about what you can do for others."

It's important for all citizens to see that they have a responsibility to something or someone other than themselves. We owe others, they don't owe us. We owe our country, our country doesn't owe us. We owe our parents, our parents don't owe us. This list could go on and on. The point is clear: it's a basic truth of life that we deserve nothing and owe everything.

In commenting on the meltdown on today's college campuses after the 2016 election, Robby Soave wrote in a piece for *Reason*, "I don't blame students for being really, really upset about Trump's win. I know plenty of mentally stable, not-at-all-coddled people who were similarly upset. But they all still went in to work on Wednesday. Life goes on."[1]

Well said. Even though I likely disagree with Mr. Soave's politics, I agree with his emphasis on telling a generation of young Americans to get a grip and get on with it. Many of us on the other side of the political aisle were equally upset with the elections of Clinton and Obama, but we didn't curl up in a fetal position in the middle of the campus green and demand goats to pet and puppies to cuddle.

Regardless of the nightly news, there is one simple fact of life: we are still in charge of our lives. There is still a job that must be performed, and when someone fails because the work is risky or uncomfortable they are selfishly imposing their workload on someone else who has to pick up those neglected duties. There are still classes that must be attended. There are still lectures to be taught. There are still debates to be had. There are still degrees to be earned. And there are still rooms to be cleaned and dishes to be washed.

Stuff happens. Dishes get dirty. Every day brings its setbacks and struggles, but the fact is that these challenges do not absolve us of our responsibilities. Life must go on. Those who suck it up and do their jobs are the adults in the room. Those who don't are akin to children controlled by someone else who does it for them.

Set Your Alarm

Chuck Swindoll, chancellor of Dallas Theological Seminary, once said, "I am convinced that life is 10% what happens to me and 90% of how I react to it."[2] The attitude with which we approach our responsibilities will tell the story of who we are and who we will become.

Responsibility is to an adult what water is to an ocean. Just as an ocean cannot exist without water, being an adult is impossible without taking responsibility.

Taking ownership rather than placing blame is a nonnegotiable step to maturity. Refusing to do so is perpetual adolescence.

Paul wrote, "For even when we were with you, we gave you this rule: 'The one who is unwilling to work shall not eat.'"[3] It is clear that he isn't speaking to the 1 percent who are unable to care for themselves, but to the 99 percent who have the ability and responsibility to take care of things. Rather than living off of others, the Thessalonians were expected to work and become a functional part of the community in which they lived.

Adults don't just accept responsibility—they actively seek it out. They don't dodge it. They see it not only as necessary for survival, but also as an opportunity. This is an attitude of dedication and determination. Whining is not an option. Wants give way to needs. Convenience is overcome by conviction and commitment.

There is a real world outside of Mom and Dad's basement. It is often a place that is harsh and unforgiving. Irresponsibility is judged, not excused. Feelings don't trump facts. There are no puppies to cuddle or goats to pet. There is work to be done. Those who do it make a difference. Those who don't are quickly forgotten.

Rather than resting comfortably in what feels safe, an adult assesses the facts, takes charge, and moves forward, taking personal responsibility to make something happen.

The junk of life does not dictate who we are. We are who we are not because of what the circumstances did to us, but, rather, because of what we did with the hand we were dealt.

The words "I just can't" give way to "I must."

It boils down to some simple life lessons.

Focus on what you have to give to the world rather than what you think the world should give you. It isn't about what you can get. It's about what you can give.

Discipline yourself. You will never get on the field or on the court if you don't go to practice, memorize the plays, pay attention to the coach, learn the rules of the game, and do what you're told. Armchair quarterbacks stay at home in the La-Z-Boy. Real athletes do their jobs, even when they don't like it, and especially when they might think they can't. That's why they get playing time.

Take care of what you do have rather than constantly worrying about what you don't. Take care of your own stuff rather than coveting the stuff of others. It's not about the 1 percent; it's about you.

Focus on what you can give, not what you can get. Whether it is giving time and money to your church, volunteering for Habitat for Humanity, or becoming a Big Brother or Sister, give! Giving is never wasted. Giving always bears positive fruit. Throwing money at technology and toys ends in buyer's remorse. It never satisfies. Giving always comes with a reward rather than regret. Stop wasting time and money on yourself. Give!

Make good choices. In reality, this is the core of what it means to be a human being. Choice is what distinguishes you from an animal. Choice is the contrast between being the *imago Dei* (the image of God) and a dog. It's the difference between freedom and bondage. Domesticated animals are confined. They are not free. They may be safe, but they make few choices. A responsible, thinking adult, on the other hand, expands her world with each wise choice she makes. This is the definition of what it means to "pursue happiness." It is the definition of what we mean by "life and liberty." Adults make choices between good and evil, freedom and slavery, and innocence and corruption. Being an adult means you can choose. Make good choices.

Stop blaming others. It's not about intersectionality. It's not about critical race theory. It's not about someone else's privilege. It's not about them; it's about you. You never break the cycle of sin by looking out the window. You only break it by looking in the mirror. Revival never starts by focusing on everyone else. It always starts with you.

Stop talking and listen. You don't have all the answers. Whether you are twenty-five or fifty-two, those who are a bit older than you are often a lot wiser than you. Don't talk *at* them, listen *to* them. If you want to become an adult, listen to one. Stop the chronological snobbery. The old ideas are often the best ideas. They have stood the test of time for a reason. Grandma and Grandpa might actually know something. Listen!

Test everything. Laziness accepts what is popular. It goes with the flow and celebrates the fad. Responsibility, on the other hand, questions everything. Is it true? Is it false? You are a rational, thinking human being. Use your brain. Always hold emotionally laden arguments at arm's length. Do the necessary homework. Find the facts. Laziness and emotion are deadly bedfellows.

One of the greatest gifts we have ever been given is the gift of responsibility. Responsibility is the gift of choice. It is the gift of freedom. It is the gift of service over selfishness. It is the gift of rationality over emotion and facts over feelings. It is the gift of adulthood over adolescence.

Where laziness ultimately leads to regrets, responsibility and determination lead to results. Assuming responsibility sets the stage not only to fulfill the requirements but to excel beyond that which is expected. This is what is implied in becoming a "responsible adult."

Plates Ready

All the people in the world who have become "success stories" have one thing in common: they chose to think for themselves and act accordingly. They didn't blame or deflect. They assumed responsibility. It was about them and not about everyone else. Rather than expecting someone else to do it, they took control of whatever situation they found themselves in and solved problems for themselves.

The apostle Paul wrote that continuing to do what is good and what is right will not fail to produce a result. He wrote, "Let us not become weary in doing good, for at the proper time we will reap a harvest if we do not give up."[4] These words have stood the test of time for nearly two thousand years. We might be wise to listen and learn from them. Good results will come if we choose to do good, take responsibility, and look at work as an opportunity rather than a curse.

In his book *Every Good Endeavor: Connecting Your Work to God's Work*, Tim Keller hits the nail on the head: "The biblical view of these matters is utterly different [then today's messaging on work and responsibility]. Work of all kinds, whether with the hands or the mind, evidences our dignity as human beings—because it reflects the image of God the Creator in us."

For anything to be reaped in the long run, something must be sown.

Sowing good ideas, good behaviors, good habits, and good choices in our daily routine bears positive fruit. Meanwhile, bad habits and choices bear rotten fruit. One seed bears a crop of more opportunity, the other leads to more outside control.

A life marked by constantly looking for a handout is not a life worth living. Such an existence is boring rather than beautiful. It is an abuse of the goodwill and hard work of others. It is selfish and insular. It is a life that tends to be demanding and arrogant rather than humble and grateful. It is the difference between an armchair quarterback sitting in Mom and Dad's basement and a real athlete who is actually on the field of play.

Responsibility comes at a cost. It is not cheap. It requires time. It demands effort. It requires commitment and sacrifice. Responsibility will often cost comfort. It may even cost you your safety. In his *Chronicles of Narnia*, C.S. Lewis writes that the great lion Aslan was not safe but he was good. So it is with the choice to take responsibility. Responsibility isn't supposed to be safe, but good. And the things in life that are truly good often cost the most, both in terms of work expended and risk to our own comfort. They are never free.

A lack of responsibility, however, costs even more than the best things life has to offer. A lack of responsibility can cost you your reputation. A lack of responsibility will leave you hungry. A lack of responsibility will leave you wanting without having. It will leave you regretting what could have been.

Jordan Peterson aptly worded growing into adulthood with the following insight:

> To stand up straight with your shoulders back is to accept the terrible responsibility of life, with eyes wide open. It means deciding to voluntarily transform the chaos of potential into the realities of habitual order. It means adopting the burden of self-conscious vulnerability and accepting the end of the unconscious paradise of childhood, where finitude and mortality are only dimly comprehended. It means willingly undertaking the necessary sacrifices to generate a productive and meaningful reality (it means acting to please God, in the ancient language).[5]

Ultimately, plates don't have legs. They pile up on the table until someone chooses to take care of the mess.

Pick up the plate and clean it. The choice is yours, and the condition of the kitchen is on you. It's your responsibility.

Don't Fall in the Pool

"You will never find a truly happy self-centered person.
They simply don't exist."

—Zig Ziglar

A Costly Selfie

The first recorded selfie fatality was in 2011. Three teenage girls were tragically struck by a train in Utah while taking a selfie on a railroad track. Unfortunately, that wasn't the last selfie fatality. There have been several selfie-related deaths since 2011. In 2014, thirty-three thousand people were injured in cell phone–related vehicle accidents, some of which were from selfies.[1] The most noted of such accidents are ones like the woman who was gored by a bison in Yellowstone while taking a selfie and the multiple people who have fallen from cliffs in Yosemite while doing the same.

Selfies have become a routine part of life with the advent of the smartphone. This makes the phenomenon fairly new. But at least one tragic selfie, rooted in Greek mythology, transcends the ages. I'm speaking of the tale of Narcissus.

Narcissus was the son of the river god Cephissus. He was an avid hunter who spent much of his time hiking the foothills of Mount Olympus, and was known for being extremely handsome. As he hunted and traversed the forest, many goddesses of Greek mythology fell in love with him, but he always spurned their love, leaving in his wake uncounted frustrated and broken hearts. One particular nymph, whose name was Echo, pined after Narcissus and pursued him relentlessly. As he did to all others, Narcissus pushed her away, leaving her to roam the wilderness calling out for him to return her affection. (Another story for another day, but the legend has it that this is the origin of echoes.)

Well, one day, upon hearing what had happened to Echo, Nemesis, the goddess of retribution and revenge, punished Narcissus. Following one of Narcissus's hunts, Nemesis lured Narcissus to a calm, clear pool carved out of a bend of a river. Exhausted, Narcissus stooped down to take a drink and was stunned to see his own reflection. Captivated, Narcissus gazed at his image. "Ah," he said to himself, "not Bacchus, Apollo, or even Zeus in all their glory surpass such allure as mine."

As time went by, Narcissus could not pull himself away. He just stayed by the river's edge, staring at his own reflection. Day after day, he hovered over the pool, gazing at himself. Weeks passed, and Narcissus became so self-infatuated that he forgot to think of anything else, even food or rest. He became emaciated, lost his color, his vigor, and his strength, until finally, in one last attempt to preserve his own fading beauty, Narcissus reached out to embrace his reflection in the pool.

He slipped, fell in, and drowned.

In love with himself, Narcissus died, leaving nothing but the faint hint of Echo's voice in a distant valley as she mourned the loss of such wasted beauty.

A bizarre story that contains a cautionary tale. In some ways, Narcissus tells the story of the deadly selfie.

A present-day Narcissus would fill up his phone's memory, quickly snapping selfies of himself. You've probably picked this up or already know the background, but the legend of Narcissus is where we get the terms narcissism and narcissist.

Simply stated, a narcissist is someone who is full of himself, often at the expense of others. In the discipline of psychology, narcissism falls along a spectrum of myopic self-infatuation and self-glorification.

This story came to mind recently when I was confronted by a young scholar who fancied himself my intellectual superior. He took great pride in his progressive ideas and disagreed with my antiquated "conservative" thinking. "The problem with you conservatives," he said, "is that you are arrogant. You think you have all the answers. You think you are always right."

Though I didn't tell him this, my young acquaintance reversed the proper attributes of the two camps. The difference between conservatives and progressives is not that conservatives think they're right and progressives don't. To the contrary, any healthy debate presupposes that one person believes his or her ideas are right while contending that another person's ideas are wrong. By definition, a disagreement assumes mutual dissent.

Common sense (as well as *Webster's Dictionary*) tells us a dispute involves arguing one thesis or idea against another. Both sides think they have the correct answer. Both are confident in the accuracy of their position. Both believe the other person's ideas are mistaken.

It's OK to have differing opinions. In fact, the very existence of argument and debate presupposes mutual disagreement. But it is also assumed that both sides think they are right.

Wouldn't it be a silly waste of breath to disagree if we had no confidence in the "rightness" of our own position and the consequent "wrongness" of opposing views?

Surely we can agree that both progressives and conservatives are equally confident in thinking they have the better ideas. It seems obvious that my young friend who claimed to be "right" in criticizing me for claiming to be "right" needed to remember that one accusing finger pointed at others is often outnumbered by several fingers pointed back at oneself.

It isn't the degree of confidence that distinguishes one "believer" from another, but rather the source of confidence. The progressive, like my young friend, claims there is no final answer. All truths are merely the consequence of social constructs and human preference. People are the source of their own truth. The conservative, on the other hand, disagrees, saying truth is bigger than this. It is an objective fact beyond our ability to create. It is out there. It is real. It is given from above and revealed through the heart. Thus, the real difference is that one man claims to be the source of truth while the other claims to be its recipient. This is the major difference between the conservative and the progressive worldview. One claims there is no truth outside of his subjective whims, and that's the truth. The other admits that truth exists and admits it's his job to find it rather than deny it.

Now, a question (or two or three):

Why is it arrogant for me to say, "I don't have all the answers, but I believe there is one," and yet humble for my young challenger to proclaim with narcissistic confidence, "There is no final answer. Truth is what I decide it is. I am the final judge. I am the ultimate arbiter of what is right and wrong, true and false, beautiful and ugly"?

This young man's comments take us back to the old Greek tale.

Is it possible that my detractor might have done well to set aside his apparent chronological snobbery for just a second or two and consider the story of Narcissus? As this smarter-than-thou young man stands at the edge of today's political pool staring lovingly at his own image, his own opinions, his own preferences, and his own desires, perhaps he would do well to ask himself if that image he is reaching out to embrace is really the exemplar of humility he fancies it to be.

Are conservatives guilty of believing they are always "right" any more than progressives? Maybe our progressive critics would do well to take a humble look in the mirror and remember that it isn't arrogant to fall in love with something bigger than yourself.

The hope, change, and transformation so many of us long for goes beyond the political arena of progressives versus conservatives. Political animus is only a symptom of the disease.

Debating differing opinions isn't the issue. That's actually healthy. The disease plaguing our culture is that we have completely abandoned any objective standard for deciding who's wrong and who's right in private disputes or public debate. In fact, we disparage the very concept of anything being objectively right and claim that such thinking is merely the power play of white privilege, intersectionality, or toxic masculinity.

My young challenger had only the intensity of his feelings to refute me. His argument was bereft of anything that even remotely resembled an interest in reality or facts. His worldview lacked any respect for foundational and objective truths. As my favorite author, C. S. Lewis, said, "He had no measuring rod outside of that which he wanted to measure so he could do no measuring."

Truth is an objective reality. It transcends our feelings and emotions. It is self-evident and endures the test of time. It is immutable and doesn't bend with political power or cultural fads. We don't create truth. We pursue it, find it, submit to it, and learn from it. We don't change truth. Truth changes us.

The consequences of abandoning truth have had a devastating effect on our culture and on the way we live our daily lives. Our nation's schools are falling further and further behind other countries on nearly every measure and every scorecard. Women have lost their privacy, their dignity, and even their identity at the hands of those who deny the truth of what it means to be a female. Children have lost their childhood, serving now as pawns in an ugly game of social engineering. Freedom of speech is mocked. Religious freedom is lost. Socialism is on the rise, while constitutional liberty is maligned. It seems the list is nearly endless.

But if we dig deeper into this cultural rush to disparage and disregard truth, what we find is that it's actually more a rejection of the source of truth than it is a denial of truth's existence.

An objective truth has to come from somewhere beyond the individual. It is more than just a collection of personal opinions. As I have said previously, truth is true even if no one believes it, and falsehood is false even if everyone believes. Truth is just true, and that's the end of it. Truth doesn't care about your opinions.

This is why Lady Justice is blind. She knows the case cannot be judged by her feelings or emotions. Truth can only be found and justice can only be administered when she blinds herself to the emotions of the case and lets the facts speak for themselves.

The Declaration of Independence suggests something similar. Truth is bestowed upon us by our Creator, not made up by a bunch of elite oligarchs dressed in black robes. Truth is not a construct of a king, nor is it the product of public consensus. Truth is revealed from above, not made up from within.

Since the founding of America, the self-evident truths and unalienable rights that form the building blocks of our society have found their source in God and the Bible. And rejection of this foundation goes hand in glove with the rejection of objective truth and the consequent loss of such rights and freedoms.

We all need to find an explanation for the reality in which we live, and that explanation must come from somewhere other than ourselves.

In the discussion with my young scholar friend, my source of truth was not myself, but something bigger, better, and wiser than me. My friend's source was himself.

Himself.

Though I had more education, experience, and sources, I still did not, nor would I ever, believe that I could produce a truth that explains the reality of this world from within my fallible self. And yet progressives proclaim that they, mere mortals, know more than all of those who have gone before them and more than even God himself. They are the ones we've been waiting for and they are the change we seek. They can stem the ocean's tide, calm the nation's storms, and control the world's climate. They can redefine biology and ignore genetics. Through their social programs, they can eliminate the natural distinction between men and women while they cleanse men of their "toxicity."

Can you spell narcissistic?

Progressive narcissism is not limited to the classroom; it's a worldview that many Americans share. Truth has been beheaded on the guillotine of the left's revolution, and freedom's blood flows in the streets of every area of life. Each and every person who proclaims that it doesn't matter what you believe as long as it works for you mimics the left's relativism. By rejecting anything outside of themselves, they hope to turn America into a nation of narcissists.

But this is far worse than the vanity of Narcissus, for this is not the stuff of Greek mythology. It is real. These people who claim to be God walk and talk among us as living, breathing, actual human beings. This is the arrogance our colleges have inculcated in our students. This is what public education has given us.

The challenge of adulting becomes even greater when you've been told to ignore actual adults who might have a thing or two to teach you. Call me crazy, but pretending you are smarter than everyone who is two days older than you and that your feelings matter more than your elders' antiquated facts is not the recipe for humility.

Educated to Be a Narcissist

In the early 1900s, G. K. Chesterton spoke of the unavoidable consequences of denying God as our Creator and worshipping science above the sacred. Observing that the naturalists of his day were only too willing to turn their science into a philosophy and then impose their new religion upon all of culture with near fanatic zeal, Chesterton said, "I never said a word against eminent men of science. What I complain of is a vague, popular philosophy which supposes itself to be scientific when it is really nothing but a sort of new religion and an uncommonly nasty one."

Recognizing that science could never presume to compete in the moral arena of theology and philosophy, Chesterton went further: "To mix science up with philosophy is only to produce a philosophy that has lost all its ideal value and a science that has lost all its practical value. It is for my private physician to tell me whether this or that food will kill me. It is for my private philosopher to tell me whether I ought to be killed."

Chesterton knew science could answer the questions of mathematics and medicine, but he was likewise keenly aware it had nothing at all to say about meaning and morality. He warned that scientific "progress" unrestrained by sacred principles was fraught with dangers. "Survival of the fittest," he contended, may be an interesting academic discussion when applied to a vegetable, an animal, or a mineral, but when practiced on people, its consequences are nothing short of horrifying.

Lewis also spoke forthrightly of Western society's diminishment of God while elevating man and technology to fill the void. Predicting the rise of what he and others labeled "scientism," where naturalism and materialism would be uncritically elevated to the status of a religion, Lewis warned of a dystopia where public policy and even moral and religious beliefs would be dictated by professors and politicians only too eager to assume the role of our new cultural high priests.

In his novel *That Hideous Strength*, Lewis asks the reader to consider an obvious question: after two world wars in which scientism has brought us the "advancements" of eugenics and the mass slaughter of millions of people via poisonous gas, rapid-fire machine guns, ballistic rockets, and atomic bombs, how is our new man-made god working for us?

"The physical sciences, good and innocent in themselves, [have] already . . . begun to be warped," said Lewis. "[They have] been subtly maneuvered in a certain direction. Despair of objective truth [has] been increasingly insinuated into [scientism]; indifference and a concentration upon mere power [and personal despair] have been the result." Lewis knew the struggle by the "fittest" for power and survival, when unhampered by any objective moral restraint, would always lead to the nightmare of Orwellian rule and self-destruction rather than the paradise promised by his professorial peers, and he cautioned his readers accordingly.

The list of those warning of the inevitable consequences of worshipping the created rather than the Creator is long. Chesterton, Lewis, J. R. R. Tolkien, T. S. Eliot, and many more, both before and after them, all knew that when man reverses the equation of Creator and created and denies God as his origin, humanity suffers dire consequences.

Chuck Colson, the late founder of the Colson Center for Christian Worldview, summarized it well: "Our origin determines our destiny. It tells us who we are, why we are here, and how we should order our lives together in society. Our view of origins shapes our understanding of ethics, law, [life, and even the end of life]. . . . Whether we start with the assumption that we are creatures of a personal God or that we are products of a mindless process, a whole network of consequences follows, and these consequences diverge dramatically."

If we are the intentional design of an intelligent creator, then we have a purpose, a destiny, and a way in which to live our lives in order to fulfill that purpose. If we are nothing more than products of happenstance and chance, then we have no ultimate purpose, no meaning, and no standard to guide the way we are to live or die. Morality becomes meaningless, and right and wrong are nothing more than power plays and social constructs. And who has more power over life and death than a man who stands alone in a room holding a noose or a bottle of pills?

Lewis, Chesterton, and Colson all warned of this brave new world where material comforts are all that matter; a world where all claims of moral truth are considered suspect; a world where we should "eat, drink, and be merry for tomorrow we may die." They knew that when we believe in the god we see in the mirror more than the God we see in the Bible, little is left for us at the end of days but to rise up and join with well-known celebrity chef Anthony Bourdain and a host of others in singing with sardonic resonance and sad self-deception, "Suicide is painless."

To move toward adulthood and begin to be men and women of integrity, all of us must shake off the self-worship and arrogance that dominates our public schools and universities. If you think you are god, there is nothing for you to learn and there is nothing you cannot and should not do. "Not even Bacchus, Apollo, or Zeus in all their glory surpass such allure as yours."

The River's Edge

Back to Narcissus. Being lured to a still, calm pool along the river, our young Greek hero walked to the water's edge and looked down to gaze at his own reflection. His arrogance consumed him. He drowned.

He is the poster child of the first fatal selfie.

Today we stand on the edge of the proverbial pool, mesmerized by our own image as much as a Greek god, if not more so.

From our first day in preschool to the time we graduate college, we have been taught that we define everything. Life. Liberty. Male. Female. Choice. Freedom. Fascism. Morality. Justice. We are the ones we've been waiting for. We are the change we seek. We decide. We define. And no one has the right to challenge our feelings or constructs.

We have all been taught to deny Copernicus. Philosophically and theologically, we are geocentrists. We deny heliocentrism. Declaring there is no Son (yes, I spelled that right), we declare ourselves to be the center of the universe.

But we can change, as we remain human beings with free minds and souls. We can look to the wisdom of the ages for answers rather than being content with the immaturity and foolishness of the new and the woke. While helicopter parenting and participation trophies may have brought us to the river's edge, we can still choose differently.

Stop the selfies.

Stop gazing at your reflection.

Listen to that still small voice echoing off in the distance, and step back.

You are not God.

Get up and turn away.

Don't fall in the pool.

Pack Jumper Cables

"Nothing good comes cheaply so we shouldn't be surprised when we meet the hard while going for the best. Hard times are not quit times."

—Terry Mark

Life's Not a Hallmark Movie

Too often, we have a misguided idea of how life will be.

We think in terms of movies, Hollywood-style "and they lived happily ever after." The false sense of easy waters, sailing off each day into a place of tranquility. But crashing waves and storms always come. They are often relentless. Life can, and will, go off-script in the blink of an eye. The key question is simple: Are we prepared?

I was once told a story about a graduate who was given a multitude of gifts following his graduation from high school. Family and friends gathered together to celebrate his achievement and graciously blessed him with many presents, and he was thankful for all of them. He most definitely appreciated the cash; it certainly did not go unspent. But, of all the gifts he received celebrating his graduation, the one he would grow to appreciate the most would be the one he questioned the most upon receipt—jumper cables.

"Why in the world would someone give jumper cables as a graduation gift?" the young man thought to himself as he smiled and thanked the gift's giver. But this gift would be the one that he would never forget, one he would use for years down the road.

The jumper cables were given by someone with a long-term perspective. Money and gift cards were more attractive gifts, sure to be appreciated by anyone. But the man who gave the jumper cables knew the difference between wants and needs. He understood that a day would come when this young graduate would need the very thing that would keep him from being stranded. It was a gift that no one else even considered giving.

The jumper cables proved their worth several times over. On multiple occasions, the graduate found himself stuck—the victim of the mechanical difficulties anyone who drives an older car is sure to understand. When a dead battery threatened to stop him dead in his tracks, a questionable gift from years earlier became the best gift of all. Long after the cash was spent and gone, there were many times when he was truly grateful he had the jumper cables.

The cables were what he needed in times of crisis. They kept him moving. They gave him a degree of independence and some measure of freedom. Rather than having to wait for a tow truck to come to his rescue, all he had to do was flag down a friend with a working car and battery, get out his cables, and solve his own problems.

The cables also gave him the means to stay on task and accomplish the normal, mundane tasks of life. Like the time right after he bought his first home and his lawn mower wouldn't start—he pulled out those cables and jump-started the mower.

They also gave him what he needed to help others. He couldn't count the times he used those cables in the heat of summer, cold of winter, during torrential rain or scorching sun to help others who weren't prepared themselves.

The moral of this story is obvious. The greatest gifts we are given are often the ones that we may not understand when we receive them. The gifts that carry lasting value are the ones that rarely catch our eye at first glance. We really didn't "want" them. But later on they bring a sigh of relief when we need them most. Those gifts are priceless, because they meet a need we may not have seen coming.

Wisdom to face situations that we cannot fathom—the crises in life that we didn't see coming—is a gift that is often underappreciated. An umbrella that gives shelter when the rain pours is never truly appreciated until the storm begins. Gloves are scoffed at until frostbite begins to set in. A flashlight seems cheap until the power goes out and you are left in the dark.

And the same can be said for jumper cables.

The Real World . . . of Adulthood

Despite living in a world saturated with reality television, all of us seem to find ourselves further removed from reality than any culture preceding us.

Ironic, isn't it?

Real life presents a series of trials and afflictions, times of sorrow and suffering that frankly aren't all that entertaining.

Solomon admitted as much when writing Ecclesiastes. The opening of the third chapter points to the highs and lows in life. Solomon wrote that there is "a time to be born and a time to die, a time to plant and a time to uproot, a time to kill and a time to heal, a time to tear down and a time to build, a time to weep and a time to laugh, a time to mourn and a time to dance."[1] Or as the Byrds sang in 1965: "There is a season, turn, turn, turn. And a time to every purpose, under heaven."

Such words are a reminder that life can be hard at times. There are difficult situations that must be faced, tumultuous seasons that must be endured, and struggles and sorrows that are common to all people, regardless of their station. A day of intense pain can come immediately after one of great joy. And generally speaking, things will not go as planned.

Though we are taught to plan out our lives to the smallest detail, we are rarely taught what to do and how to react when those plans don't work or when achieving our goals becomes a longer process than initially anticipated.

A friend who is a pastor once shared a story with me. When he was new in the ministry, he would sit down on Sunday nights and plan out his week. He had many competing duties as part of his job, so to ensure he accomplished what "needed" to be done, he assembled a meticulous and detailed list. He charted who needed to be visited, what meetings he needed to attend, time for planning and studying for sermons, and all the other demands of being a pastor. Without fail, every Monday brought something unplanned and unscripted that had to be dealt with immediately. From there, the schedule would often derail quickly.

Initially, the constant reconfiguration of the schedule was a source of angst for the young pastor. Each week, he would end up with five to ten things that remained unfinished, overloading the following week's demands. Not a single week went according to his script.

When the pastor began to understand that these changes were just a part of life, he adjusted better to the interruptions. He gained perspective through it all, realizing that a seasoned professional—a mature adult—learns to manage his planner rather than let his planner manage him.

Sickness interrupts what we thought would be a time of health. A broken appliance reaches into our savings account, thwarting our vacation plans. A traffic jam causes us to be late. Fires, tornadoes, and floods can wipe away all sense of stability at a moment's notice. Relationships that seemed destined to last a lifetime end prematurely due to distance, lack of time, disagreements, controversy, or simply growing apart. The death of a loved one or a friend confronts us with a sense of unexpected grief and sorrow. Jobs can lead to a relocation that uproots us from what we thought would be our forever home. And some days, the car won't start.

As Robert Burns said,

> But mouse, you are not alone,
> In proving foresight may be in vain;
> The best laid schemes of mice

And men go often askew,
And leave us nothing but grief,
For the promised joy!

Quitters Quit

What we choose to do in response to the challenges life poses us defines us. Those who choose to give up and quit earn the opprobrium that comes with being known as a quitter. Quitting is a decision, and those who choose to quit are defined as quitters.

Quitting is a pattern that develops over the course of a lifetime, becoming easier and easier when one develops the habit of giving up on a task or a goal. After we quit something for the first time, we have much less guilt and shame about abandoning another pursuit. Rather than persevering and learning from the struggle, we grow softer when we give up.

Solomon tells us that as iron sharpens iron, one man should sharpen the other. This implies resistance. It tells us that sparks will fly and heat will be applied. A lack of conflict only dulls the sword. Paul uses a similar analogy when he tells us our workmanship will be tested and proven by fire. The apostle Peter essentially says the same when he reminds us that our character and faith will be refined by fire. It is in the heat of the difficult times that our metal is proved. Growth happens when we overcome the struggles and afflictions that life presents.

Those who consistently cower and try to run away from obstacles and struggles are those who become snowflakes. Unable to handle any heat, they melt away in selfish indignation and insignificance.

Generations ago, the thought of retreating at the first sight of struggle would have been seen as an embarrassment. Now, giving up when the going gets tough is a source of comedy, an opportunity to blame everyone else, and a chance to start our ninety-seventh new beginning in life.

Here's a spoiler: the best predictor of future behavior is always past behavior. The ninety-seventh won't be your last. There will be a ninety-eighth as soon as there is difficulty in the ninety-seventh.

Those who quit have a major aversion to being tested and are unable to face the issues that life is destined to bring. A quitter exposes that his heart was never fully committed. He is more interested in comfort than conviction. He has no courage. Being coddled as a child is more important to him than proving he's a man of character.

When did a lack of courage become a cultural good? When did a lack of fortitude become something that we champion rather than condemn?

When children throw in the towel, adults dig in. Being an adult means seeing obstacles as opportunities and ways to grow, and embracing challenges even when they seem overwhelmingly difficult. Growing up means that the days of doing what's easy and safe are given up for hard work. It means risking failure for the sake of achieving something great and good, regardless of what stands in the way.

Think about New Year's resolutions. Every year, as midnight begins to approach, we spout off a habit we hope to change in the coming weeks and months. But according to research conducted by the University of Scranton, 92 percent of people fail to live up to their resolution, giving up on the new life they envisioned for themselves. That means that only 8 percent stick to their word and see their project through. As Marcel Schwantes wrote for Inc.com, "The 8 percent have an internal compass that keeps them locked in until they reach the top of the mountain. It's a belief system of 'do whatever it takes' that is intrinsically motivated at their core."[2]

Failure to stick to New Year's resolutions may seem a trivial example, but the statistics indicate a larger trend in Western European and American culture. When the going gets tough, we quit. We commit only to the point that it is comfortable. At the first sign of discomfort, we "decommit" and move on to something more pleasant.

If a boss is too demanding, quit and go to work for a new boss until the new boss grows too demanding. "I can't do it" is the cry of our times. This attitude trickles down in a lack of cultural resolve. The story of the Little Engine That Could has become a bunch of little engines that would rather not.

Adulthood cannot be flipped on and off like a light switch. Maturity requires us to stand when the going gets difficult, to fight for something bigger than ourselves rather than pushing back under the covers, unable to deal with an imperfect world.

As Katharine Hepburn quipped in her book, "Life is hard. After all, it kills you."[3]

Though there are struggles, adults endure.

Preparing for a Storm

In September 2018, the Eastern Seaboard of the United States braced for a Category 4 hurricane. The exact time the storm would hit was uncertain. Hurricanes tend to have a mind of their own. There was no guarantee where the storm would make landfall, but that didn't prevent people up and down the coastline from preparing. North Carolina and South Carolina residents were vigilant as the storm crept towards the coastline.

Windows were boarded up. Items on the porch that could fly away were either strapped down or taken indoors. Residents hoping to stop the rising waters from rushing inside placed sandbags in front of their homes. Plans were made for where the residents would go to evacuate.

As Hurricane Florence made its way to the southeast of the United States, those in the path of the storm knew that being unprepared was not an option. Rather than leaving their homes and their lives to chance, they took action and did everything possible to prepare to weather the storm and, eventually, bounce back after the hurricane had passed.

When Florence finally made landfall at Wrightsville Beach, North Carolina, the residents had done all that they could to prepare. The storm was hitting. Now all they could do was hope that the buildings could withstand the deluge and that the preparations they had made were enough to keep their houses intact.

Jesus talked about all of this. In fact, he used the analogy of a storm to explain the importance of solid foundations in life. He said, "Therefore everyone who hears these words of mine and puts them into practice is like a wise man who built his house on the rock. The rain came down, the streams rose, and the winds blew and beat against that house; yet it did not fall, because it had its foundation on the rock."[4]

The wise builder is prepared. He chooses a solid foundation. He "hears and puts into practice." He does what is necessary in advance of the storm to withstand the floods and the winds when they strike.

But Jesus also told us the outcome of those who refuse to do this, of those who don't want to do the hard work of digging deep and breaking through to rock, those who would prefer the ease of sand. They have no foundation. "Their house will crash."[5]

Both the wise and the foolish builders experienced the difficulties of life. Hardships came. Storms raged. In fact, if you look closely at Christ's parable, identical types of storms struck each person and each house. Rains, winds, and rising streams hit both.

One stood while the other fell. The only difference between the two was the foundation upon which they were constructed. The distinction between success and failure was preparation.

Adults plan for the un-plannable by preparing. They find the right foundation for whatever life may bring. We fortify who we are and what we stand upon by "hearing and putting into practice" the wisdom of those who have dealt with storms before us. We understand that sands of popular opinion crumble. We look for the rock of time-tested truths. As a result, we endure rather than quitting when we face adversity.

Planning means finding the conviction to double down when difficulty and crisis come. Preparation not only reduces the likelihood of structural collapse and personal loss, but it also gives us the confidence to know how to rebuild when we do suffer damage.

This is the difference between hopelessness and hope. It is the difference between faith and fear. Faith is substantial. Paul says, "It is the substance of things hoped for." True faith is not built on ideological sands of feelings and fear. It is anchored deep in the self-evident "substance" of truths that do not move. True faith knows that it knows. There isn't a shadow of doubt that the rock is stable and real. Having a foundation of faith rather than fear ensures that we will stand even when life gets hard. We have hope. We are not hopeless.

Because we have prepared by "hearing and putting into practice" what the master architect and builder has told us, we don't give up. We dig in. We stand firm. We are resolute in our confidence that the foundation will hold. Saint Paul goes further when speaking about the complexities of life, the struggles and the hardships. His words give us the first line of defense when life is hard. He wrote, "We are hard pressed on every side, but we are not crushed; perplexed, but not in despair; persecuted, but not abandoned; struck down, but not destroyed."[6]

Rather than bemoaning the difficulty, Paul celebrates opportunity. Being "hard pressed" did not change the fact that he refused to be crushed. He welcomed the struggle and was not overcome by it. Paul focused on his destiny and not on despair. He knew iron sharpened iron. He welcomed the sword!

Much of life is hard, but the preparation that allows us to overcome difficulty is found in doing the work of digging deeper into the rock. Those who look for the safety and ease of "sand" will eventually crumble. Those who welcome conflict with courage will find growth and success.

A lifestyle that lacks commitment and runs from difficulties seems to be the norm rather than the exception today. One of the obvious examples is the average length of marriages and a divorce rate of nearly 50 percent. The length of time millennials commit to their given employers is another example. But job-hopping and serial marriages did not spring upon the scene out of thin air. The roots of this lack of commitment span back more than thirty years, as noted by Chuck Colson in *Christianity Today*: "Among today's young adults, the unwillingness to commit is alarming, clearly one result of the philosophies of the 1960s and '70s coming to full flower."[7]

We live in a time and culture where many have bought the lie that life is analogous to a vacation rather than a storm. Everything should be easy and comfortable. We think we should be able to lie on the beaches and play in the sand. And when something goes wrong we gripe rather than grow. We act like scared children rather than secure adults.

Growing up means seeing life's circumstances not as barriers but as steps toward the finish line. Children give up because their confidence is shallow. They run from adversity and storms because their foundation is not yet built. Adults stand strong. Their courage is deep. Their foundation is rock-solid. They run into the storm, not away from it.

Paul shouted, "But one thing I do: Forgetting what is behind and straining toward what is ahead, I press on toward the goal to win the prize for which God has called me...."

Henry David Thoreau chimed in, "However mean your life is, meet it and live it; do not shun it and call it hard names."[8]

Never curse the conflict. Relish it. For it is the obstacles of life that are ultimately the substance of life. With apologies to Plato, it is not the unexamined life that is not worth living, but the unchallenged one—for such a conflict-free life is delusional. It's a lie.

Remember that temporary afflictions are just that—they are temporary. Though it may seem like an eternity in the moment of the affliction, the struggle will pass and a new day will dawn. Rather than wallowing in pity during a struggle, rejoice in the opportunity to grow up.

Focus on where you are going, not what stands in the way. And always pack jumper cables.

Don't Argue with the Mechanic

"The truth is incontrovertible. Malice may attack it, ignorance may deride it, but in the end, there it is."

—Winston Churchill

Strange Noises

If someone mentions a car problem around men my age, someone in the group usually has a diagnosis and a fix. A friend once told the story of hearing a strange noise in the car. He had a pressing engagement and didn't have time to get it hauled to a shop. He was attending a multiple-day conference, and during conversations he had throughout the event, the story of his vehicle problems would come up. Every time he'd tell the story and try to mimic the sound the car was making, someone would offer his or her opinion on how to fix the problem.

He returned from his conference and had the car towed to a shop. He called the repair shop to tell the mechanic about the problem. By now he could not only describe what the car did and the strange noise it made, but he had a long list of conjectures as to what might be wrong. My friend knew a little about cars, so some of the opinions were checked off the list as completely incorrect, but there were a few hypotheses that seemed plausible. He told the mechanic the different possible diagnoses, and he ended the conversation with his own opinion. The mechanic responded with a simple "Thank you" and then said, "We'll get it hooked up to our computers and then get in the motor to see what the problem might be."

My friend had been given a bunch of opinions. He relayed those opinions to the mechanic. But that's just it—they were opinions. They were conjecture. In our exchange about it, he said, "I know there were at least fifteen different scenarios I discussed with others."

Out of those fifteen, how many do you think were valid? Were all fifteen opinions correct? What about even half of them? Could that one noise be explained by all these different armchair analyses?

No. Some of these opinions had to be wrong. In fact, the vast majority of them were. But some of the guys knew cars. Some had experience working on cars. Some felt very confident that they knew what was wrong. But none of them had actually looked at the car. None of them had the hard evidence. Only the mechanic knew what was real and not conjecture.

Opinions are just that, opinions, and at the end of the day, they really don't matter. You don't pay the mechanic because he has a feeling. You pay him because he knows the facts. Engines and transmissions get fixed because someone with knowledge and training tears them apart; sees the facts; assesses the damage, the wear, the tear; and then repairs or replaces the defective parts.

If my car isn't running, I really don't care how you feel about it. I want you to understand the facts and fix it.

Now, unlike members of my generation, most millennials and Gen-Zers aren't going to offer vehicle advice. But they do have their opinions on a host of issues, and the sad fact is that many of them have never been told that their feelings really don't matter and their opinions may be wrong. And if any courageous teacher ever dares to break the news to the princess that she is not the final measure of all that is right and real in the world, her parents load up in their proverbial helicopter and head off to the school to set that teacher straight. Daddy's little girl continues to be coddled. Feelings are elevated over facts. Diplomas are handed out for opinions. What could possibly go wrong?

The law of non-contradiction is quite simple and clear. When two people hold mutually exclusive views, one is wrong and the other is right, or both are wrong. But both cannot be right. For example, if we are riding together in a car and we've just driven out of Michigan and I claim we have entered Ohio, and you say, no, it's Indiana, we cannot both be right. These are mutually exclusive claims. Either one of us is right and the other is wrong, or we are both wrong because we're in Canada. The facts are the facts. Truth does not yield to emotion. You can pretend until the cows come home that because you're a Hoosier, you feel it just has to be Indiana. But that feeling doesn't matter. Ohio is Ohio and Canada is Canada. Facts don't care about your feelings.

For several decades, our educational establishment has disparaged objective truth as being closed-minded and intolerant. Over and over again we have heard the mantra, *"All paths lead to the same summit"* or *"All religions are the same."* Then there is the constant refrain of "It doesn't matter what you believe as long as it works for you." In previous chapters I have already highlighted the dangers of such radical relativism, as well as the difference between subjective truth and objective truth. This is the foundational battleground of the raging culture wars. Since we've already covered some of these ideas and terms, I will spend only a brief time here in explaining them.

To put in perspective the gravity of this situation, listen to what former Speaker of the House Paul Ryan stated when he was asked what he believed to be the greatest problem facing America. "If you ask me what the biggest problem in America is, I'm not going to tell you debt, deficits, statistics, economics—I'll tell you it's moral relativism."[1]

As you would expect, I agree in large measure with Representative Ryan. In fact, I was once asked a similar question on a national radio show. More specifically, I was asked what key stories in the news I believed were having the greatest impact on our nation, our freedoms, and our way of life. For me, the answer was and is obvious: it's feelings versus facts. One side is willing to admit certain moral facts and the possibility of objective truth, while the other wants to remake the world according to "narratives" and its subjective impressions.

This might sound a bit hyperbolic, but it's not. The reality is that the elevation of feelings over facts in our schools and our churches, as well as in our courtrooms and our Congress, is a malignant cancer that threatens the very existence of our constitutional republic. It is a Category 5 hurricane that is sweeping across our culture with such devastating force that its path of destruction widens by the day.

Feelings versus facts is one of the results of moral and ideological relativism.

Relativism is a philosophical argument grounded in the premise that there is no such thing as objective truth that governs us or our culture, but, rather, each individual or community constructs their own truths to suit their own relative needs and circumstances. Collegially stated, relativism is the idea that what is true for you may not be true for me and vice versa. There is no such thing as a consistent revealed standard. Everything is subjective to the person and the culture. The idea of "self-evident truths" being "endowed to us by our Creator" is a ruse of colonial times, male toxicity, and white privilege. Within this framework, there are no absolutes. Behind this worldview is the idea that there is no such thing as a universal truth that applies to all people and all cultures. What's important to understand is that there is, then, no such thing as a common code of conduct. There is no such thing as objective good and evil. What is just and unjust is constructed by society. It is a product of the collective. The judge is now the gang, not God.

Relativism says that what is right for one person is right for him, but if someone else believes the exact opposite, that is "right" also. It ignores the law of non-contradiction. It is summed up in the oh-so-common postmodern retort: "Whatever." In fact, if I may coin a phrase, philosophical and moral relativism is really nothing more than adolescent "whateverism." Want to steal? Whatever. Want to lie? Whatever. Want to cheat? Whatever. Want to be a woman even though you're really a man? Whatever. Want to kill babies just before they're born? Whatever. You get the point.

But at the same time, relativists can't live by their own rules because they are the first to condemn conservatives—even though conservatives' beliefs works for them. In fact, conservatives' beliefs matters so much to relativists that they must be suppressed and silenced. All of a sudden the big progressive group hug of "live and let live" turns into angry shouts: "I don't care what you believe! Your intolerance cannot be tolerated!"

If this sounds like anarchy to you, then you have more sense than so many of my academic peers who teach this pablum on our college campuses. It never ceases to amaze me how so-called scholars can actually maintain a straight face when they say stuff like, "I am sure nothing is sure. I know nothing can be known. And I am absolutely confident there are no absolutes."

Anyway, I digress. The bottom line is that relativism is the rejection of any absolute truth.

Absolute truth is a description of reality in which truth isn't flexible or fluid. It doesn't bend to whims of politics or power. It isn't subject to change just because of someone's feelings. I have already mentioned this quote from Os Guinness's book, *Time for Truth*, but it bears repeating over and over again: "Truth is true even if no one believes it and falsehood is false even if everyone believes it. Truth is true and that's just the end of it." This worldview of Guinness (as well as that of nearly every theologian and philosopher in the course of human history up until, oh, let's say, the last five decades) argues that there is always a measuring rod outside of those things being measured and that measuring rod is truth. Truth is immutable. It is found in revelation and natural law. It is self-evident but not self-referential. It is endowed by God and not created by the consensus of the gang. In most contexts, especially in the West, absolute truth is contained in the teachings of the Judeo-Christian ethic—that is, of God and the Bible.

The apostle Paul, however, tells us in his Letter to the Romans that "the truth of God is written on every human heart." In other words, truth doesn't have to be limited to just the Bible. We see absolute truth in nature, in science, in mathematics, and in the common moral assumptions we hold as human beings.

All of us (liberals and progressives alike) assume the existence of these absolutes. In fact, we couldn't live life in any normal capacity without them.

It's an absolute that $2 + 2 = 4$. The term "absolute" is given to numbers to show that the claims we make by using them are irrefutable and real. The law of gravity is another absolute. What goes up will come down. Throw a ball up in the air, and you know what it is going to do.

And hopefully we can all agree that rape and slavery are absolutely wrong. Even though we can't test such a claim in a test tube, we know it is irrefutably and immutably true. It is written on our hearts.

The denial of absolute truth is a denial of logic. In order to say there are no absolutes, you have to claim that it is absolutely true that there are no absolutes. A self-refuting claim if there ever was one.

Denial of absolutes is also a denial of God. It is essentially the replaying of the original sin cited in the book of Genesis, where we join with Adam and Eve in declaring that we don't need God any longer to tell us what is good and evil, true and false, or right and wrong. To the contrary, we have become "as gods," knowing and defining everything for ourselves.

Dr. Craig Mitchell, a philosophy professor at Southwestern Baptist Theological Seminary and the University of Texas at Arlington, writes about our culture's slow fade into relativism.[2] He contends that there have been three overarching frameworks in the history of the Western world, three movements, or metanarratives, under which all others fall.

He describes the first phase as the beginning of human history up to the 1600s and the rise of humanism and the Enlightenment. He labels this first stage premodernity. In the premodern world, truth was supernatural. Truth was a revelation, not a construct. It was transcendent. Its source was God. The monotheistic beliefs of Judaism and Christianity are obvious examples of this. But premodern assumptions of truth were pervasive throughout all ancient cultures. Prior to the Enlightenment, it was assumed that truth came from either the gods or God. It was given from above. It wasn't made up by you or me.

Within the premodern framework, truth was considered absolute and rooted in an outside source. It also corresponded with reality. It was an accurate reflection of how the world, the cosmos, and all things therein worked.

Interestingly, this premodern assumption as the context for Christianity was a hermeneutic of trust, meaning the Bible was looked at as the source of truth and as trustworthy. It was revealed. It was immutable. It was not subject to change. God's written revelation served as our measuring rod and trump card on all of life and all of living.

After premodernity, however, comes modernity. If the hermeneutic of the premoderns was "Trust the supernatural," the hermeneutic of the moderns was "Trust the simply natural." In other words, if you can't taste, touch it, and see it, then doubt it. Suspicion rushed in to fill the vacuum left by the death of faith. Scientism replaced God as the source of all truth. Before modernity, the supernatural claims of the Bible were accepted as fact, but following on the heels of the Enlightenment, skepticism replaced belief. And because the argument was that you couldn't test the moral claims of religion in a test tube, Christianity's concepts of personal responsibility, sin, ethics, and justice were rejected.

This would pretty much be the state of affairs in Western culture until the 1950s. But then the foundation of truth shifted again. The march of human history had gone from premodernity and its trust in the supernatural, to modernity and its trust in the simply natural, to the twentieth century and the birth of postmodernity and its confidence, not in the supernatural, or the simply natural, but in the Übermensch, the Superman. In this brave new world, the individual rises up as the only source of truth and squashes even the empirical facts of the five senses. Everything is subjective. Nothing is objective. Everything is constructed. Nothing is revealed.

In the case of premodernity, truth came from God and therefore applied to all mankind. In modernity, truth was still considered universal, but was only knowable through science and empirical study. In postmodernity, truth became little more than subjective feelings and was knowable only to and by the individual. There is no such thing as Truth with a capital *T*, but only subjective lowercase "truths" that are fluid from individual to individual. When culture commentators speak of postmodernity, this is what they are referencing: a time when truth and morality are not seen as coming from any source other than themselves. Arthur W. Pink, an English Bible teacher speaking in the last half of the twentieth century, sums it up well: "Ours is peculiarly an age of irreverence, and as the consequence, the spirit of lawlessness, which brooks no restraint and which is desirous of casting off everything which interferes with the free course of self-will, is rapidly engulfing the earth like some giant tidal wave."

In postmodernity, we are the Übermensch, the Supermen. We define what is true and false. We don't need science and we surely don't need God. As Barack Obama said during his rise to the presidency in 2008, "We are the ones we've been waiting for. We are the change we seek." In other words, we are gods!

The heart of the snowflake rebellion, of trigger warnings and microaggressions, of safe spaces and speech codes, is built on the premise of relativism. What is happening in our universities is the result of teaching multiple generations to believe that the way they feel matters far more than the facts, and that what they hear is far more important than what they have been told. Maybe there's some merit to the optimistic idea that the victims of the vampire are finally waking up to see it as the monster it is, but it is futile to believe that either the broken test tubes of modernity or the shifting sands of postmodernity lend themselves to a viable solution.

How can we expect to regain our cultural footing if there is no rock of truth upon which to stand? With sand and shattered glass as our building material, it should surprise no one that our house is crumbling.

Our Feelings Are Killing Us

Our cultural foundation has no structural integrity. And what makes matters even worse is that there is a subterranean river tearing away at it even as we speak, eroding it and weakening it by the minute. The societal structure that is paramount to acting and living as an adult is like the Roman Colosseum of old: cracked, weak, and ready to fall.

Our culture has become obsessed with bread and circuses. As long as our bellies are full and our intellects are numb, we march along like mindless lemmings toward our own destruction. The infatuation with socialism, climate change, the name-it-claim-it ontology of trans identity, the suppression of free speech on our college campuses—all of this is the result of elevating feelings over facts. Left unchecked, it will continue to destroy anything that's left of a free society and a free people.

In the 1992 case of *Planned Parenthood v. Casey*, former Supreme Court justice Anthony Kennedy made the definitive statement of our time that summarizes the lie of radical relativism. He stated, "At the heart of liberty is the right to define one's own concept of existence, of meaning, of the universe, and the mystery of human life."

Congratulations, you just read some of the most vacuous nonsense ever uttered from our nation's echelons of power.

How so?

Let's suppose you're a brand-new college student. You have just enrolled in your first semester at my university. You've selected an academic major. You've purchased all your textbooks. You've reviewed all your syllabi and taken note of all your assignments. Your goal of getting an undergraduate or graduate degree is now at hand. You're finally in college and you head off to class. You're ready to learn.

Now fast-forward. It's four years later. You've just completed your last finals week, and commencement day has come. You are about to graduate. The time you've been waiting for is here. The speaker is finished, and you stand with all the other graduates to approach the platform. Your name is called. The academic dean gives you your honors cord. Your family is in the audience cheering. You proudly walk across the stage toward me. We join in a vigorous handshake as I give you your long-awaited diploma and lean over and whisper in your ear, "Congratulations! You now have a degree in opinions."

After four long years of study, eight semesters of classes, countless late nights of cramming for tests, dozens upon dozens of quizzes and papers—after so much hard work, I have the audacity to hand you a diploma and essentially say, "It really doesn't matter what you believe as long as it works for you. Here is your degree in opinions."

That would be ridiculous, and the absurdity would be obvious.

We all know that you didn't go to college to major in "whatever" or to get a degree in "opinions." You didn't go "to define your own concept of existence, of meaning, of the universe, and the mystery of human life." To the contrary, you went to college to actually *learn* something.

When it comes down to it on commencement day, your opinion and "your own concept of existence" really don't matter, nor do mine. What matters is quite simple. Did you learn what was required of you?

You can't pretend to be educated if all you have is an opinion. There are indisputable truths that serve as the foundation for any meaningful college degree. Getting an education requires learning such truths, not simply holding to your opinions. To claim otherwise is just absurd.

Postmodernity and its sages, such as Justice Kennedy, argue that there is no such thing as objective truth and that all values, all morality, and all ideas of right and wrong and good or bad are merely the products of an ongoing "community narrative" or social dialogue within a "global village."

According to this mindset, truth is a construct, not a precept. It is a conversation, not a conclusion. Truth is really not true, you know. It's all a matter of opinion. We all have "the right to define [our] own concept of existence, of meaning, of the universe, and the mystery of human life."

Do we really believe this, and are we willing to live with the consequences of such bad ideas?

All of us intuitively know the foundation is weak and the building is going to fall. All of us know that if we don't get out, and soon, it is going to come crashing down and kill us.

The Mechanic Bill

Remember my friend's car problems? He had been given fifteen opinions from his friends. He took that information to the mechanic. The mechanic listened but knew that his own work would uncover the actual problem.

This expert listened to the strange noise and connected his diagnostic scanner to the car's computer. It gave him a code. The code narrowed down the list of possibilities. Next, this mechanic disassembled the motor to see what the actual problem was for himself. Once he came up with a diagnosis to the problem, he got to work fixing it.

When my friend picked up his car, the mechanic told him what the real problem was. My friend could have told him that wasn't true and claimed that one of the other fifteen ideas were correct simply because he felt better about them. He could even have said it with great passion.

But none of that would have mattered, because the mechanic could show my friend a running car. No matter what my friend felt and no matter what his opinions were, the engine was real, and it had real problems and needed real solutions. My friend's feelings weren't going to fix it, nor were the opinions of his friends. The mechanic, who actually looked at the objective truth of the matter, knew what to do. The others could go pound sand.

Truth is true even if no one believes it, and falsehood is false even if everyone believes it. The truth regarding the car was true and that's just the end of it. Truth matters. Don't argue with the mechanic.

You're Not Webster

"Words—so innocent and powerless as they are, as standing in a dictionary, how potent for good and evil they become, in the hands of one who knows how to combine them!"

—Nathaniel Hawthorne

The Field Is Already Set

Creatio ex nihilo is a Latin phrase used to describe a central theological and ontological point: creation out of nothing. It's a term that captures the central event of Genesis 1:1, "In the beginning God created..."

God created this universe and He did so out of nothing. No raw materials. Nothing in play. He and he alone set the field. As Billy Preston said, "Nothin' from nothin', leaves nothin', Ya gotta have somethin', If ya wanna be with me..."

Creatio ex nihilo is God's and God's alone. No mere creature can create from nothing as the Creator can. And no matter what you've been told, there is a God and it's not you. The world isn't clay in your hands. It's not a blank canvas. It's not whatever you want to make it.

Now, you are still capable of a great deal even though you cannot create the universe from nothing. Since you are made in the image of God as a morally aware and culpable human being, you do have creative freedom and personal responsibility. You are not a robot. Your career, for example, is something you can define and create. Likewise, your reputation is largely within your power to craft, shape, and mold. But when it comes to much of the world in which you live and work, the field is already set. The boundaries are already defined. The goals are in place. There are rules to the game. Out of bounds is out of bounds, a foul is a foul, and there is a referee who has the whistle.

Despite what B. F. Skinner says, we do have the ability to do a lot, change a lot, and create a lot. But there is also an awful lot that just is, and you have no business or power to change or redefine it. Facts are facts and that's just the end of it. No, Bill Clinton, the definition of "is" is not subject to your political agenda or sexual fancy. There are some things that just are what they are. Truth is true and falsehood is false and that *IS* just the end of it.

In the previous chapter, we talked about the warped mindset of relativism, which sees the world with you as its center. According to that maligned view of the world, you are the grand interpreter, the final authority, and the definer of all. You establish your own truths. You create your own values. You author your own rules. You decide what's good and evil, bitter and sweet, true and false, because, after all, it doesn't matter what you believe as long as it works for you. This is a worldview I called "whateverism," because anytime any value or idea is up for debate, you can simply shrug and say "whatever." This is a philosophy that essentially argues that nothing matters other than the individual and his or her personal gratification. Live and let live. After all, who is to judge?

Hopefully, you see through this charade by now and know that it is a fairy tale of dancing unicorns and leprechauns. It's simply not reality. This is a land of make-believe and pretend. Not only does it ignore the empirical facts of biology and physics, but it also ignores the reality of natural law and common sense.

For example, all of us have to admit that there are some moral truths we know to be objectively true that you can't test in a tube. I hope we can all agree that it is objectively true that rape is wrong, the Holocaust was evil, and slavery is a really bad idea. You can't "prove" any of this in a laboratory, but I think all of us can admit that we can and still do know for a fact that all of this is irrefutably wrong regardless of how someone feels about it. Feelings don't change the indisputable facts of science, and your feelings also don't change the hard, cold reality that using another person's body, buying and selling other human beings, and burning Jews in furnaces are not good things to do. After all, you can't argue with the mechanic. Some things about an engine are just true.

To repeat: On the ontological field of creation, there are some things that simply are what they are. The yard lines are down. The boundaries are set. The rule book is written. It can't be manipulated into whatever you'd like it to be. We live in a real world with established facts, and denying those facts doesn't change them. Jumping out of an airplane while shouting "I can fly" does not change or negate the law of gravity. Pretending the world is flat does not change the fact that you can still sail around it. Suggesting that the evil of rape is a social construct, rather than an absolute evil, will win you few points at the social justice warriors convention. There are absolutes. There are objective truths. And that's the truth.

The fact of the matter is that, for much of your life, you will be dealt a set of cards. And, you must play the hand you're dealt. You are black. You are white. You are Hispanic. You are Asian. You are Jewish. You are male or you are female. You are blind. You can see. You are deaf. You can hear. You are short. You are tall. These are the cards you were dealt. You can't change them. They just are. It is what it is. Play them. It's your hand.

Because so much of the field is set, all of us have to realize that the only way to win the game is to play within the established boundaries. You can't play soccer with three bases, a home plate, and a triangular field. Baseball is baseball and soccer is soccer. Both sports have a definition and a purpose. Both sports mean something. All of us must play the game we're in. Pretending basketball is hockey doesn't make it so.

One of the primary realities of the field of human existence that is being attacked and ignored right now is the definition and meaning of words. We are treating discourse and words as if they mean nothing and are as flexible and moldable as clay.

But by and large, we all know intuitively that the rules of language have been set, and indeed must be set. If we are to communicate sanely and intelligently with one another, a pony can't be a fish and a fish can't be a chicken.

The meaning of words must be objective, predictable, and enduring. Frankly, this is self-evident and irrefutable, because if it were not you couldn't read this sentence and have any hope of understanding what it says. The very nature of speaking, reading, and writing obviously assumes definitional clarity; otherwise normal daily communication would become as impossible as trying to play football without any field or ball. When it comes to a dictionary, facts matter, not your feelings. You might feel like red is a number. But it's not. You might feel like two plus two equals green. But it doesn't. You might feel that dogs are quarter horses and that your Labrador Retriever lays eggs. But she won't. In all of these examples, none of your feelings change the facts of what truly "is." Definitions matter. Your delusions don't.

Much of the derailment of truth in our culture today stems from our abuse of and disrespect for words and their meanings.

Many terms that are being thrown around today to shape our country and culture—your life and mine—are being used to deceive more than they are being used to clarify.

I'm a Liberal

Let's take the word "liberal," for example. It has a history and it has a definition. It means something.

I am an orthodox evangelical Christian and a conservative. I have been waving the banner for the conservative cause for years. But here's something that may surprise you. As a thoughtful conservative, I am, frankly, more classically liberal than many of my left-of-center progressive counterparts.

How so?

Well, it's a simple matter of definition.

The common understanding of liberalism today highlights one of those words that has been co-opted by a political agenda and twisted and turned upside down to mean the exact opposite of what it is intended to mean. It has been manipulated and redefined in the same way that a "Minister of Meaning" in some smoke-filled room in an Orwell novel might decide that bitter now means sweet and sweet now means bitter. And you and I bought the lie. We didn't have the intestinal fortitude to tell Big Brother and his minions that they were lying to us. The result is that the true definition of the word "liberal" has been all but forgotten.

As self-evident as it is, I have to repeat this for emphasis: Words mean something! As human beings, we are unique in our use of language as our primary method of communication. We debate and we argue. We make speeches and we deliver sermons. We teach lessons. We pontificate, we preach, and we proclaim. We espouse liberal and conservative ideas. Our "bigger ideas" are framed and defended with emotion, passion, anger, and indignation. We have confidence in our words, and we resist any attempt to co-op, twist, or manipulate their meanings. We defend our words with tenacity. If they deceive, we call them lies. If they embolden, we call them inspiring. If they make promises, we call them contracts. Words indeed mean something, and history shows that they have the power to build nations, define religions, inspire revolutions, defend what is true, or even hide what is false.

But in spite of such power, some words are used so frequently and frivolously that they suffer for lack of care. As a result, their roots, their origins, their intents, and their purposes are lost. Words like change and choice, green and gay, left and right, toleration, integration, and discrimination—even words like liberal and conservative, if left untended—can be used to defend concepts quite contrary and perhaps even opposite to that of their original meaning.

Now back to my claim that may have shocked you when I first said it. As an unapologetic conservative, my "liberal" credentials will stack up quite well with those of any of my contemporary peers in the academic, political, social, or religious venues of our day. Compared to nearly all of them, I am the true liberal!

I am a liberal because I believe that the best education is one that indeed liberates. It liberates us from the consequences of those things that are wrong and frees us to live within the beauty of those things that are right.

I am a liberal because of my passion for a liberal arts education. A true liberal arts education is an education driven by the hunger for answers rather than the protection of opinions, an education that is not subject to the ebb and flow of personal agendas or political fads, an education that is not afraid to put all ideas on the table because there is confidence that in the end we will embrace what is true and discard what is false.

I am a liberal because I believe in freedom—freedom of thought and expression, and the freedom to dissent from consensus. I am energized by the unapologetic pursuit of truth wherever it leads, just as I am confident in the words, "You shall know the truth, and the truth shall set you free."

I am a liberal because I believe that truth cannot be segregated into false dichotomies, but is an integrated whole. The liberally educated person recognizes that we cannot and should not separate personal life from private life, the head from the heart, fact from faith, or belief from behavior.

I am a liberal because I believe in conservation. There are ideas that are tested by time, defended by reason, validated by experience, and confirmed by revelation, and they should be conserved. We are in fact endowed by our Creator with an objective moral understanding. I believe in nature and its natural law. We do know that rape is wrong, that the Holocaust was bad, and that hatred and racism are to be reviled. Even though we cannot produce these truths in a test tube, we hold them to be self-evident laws that no human being can deny.

I am a liberal because I recognize that when we exchange the truth for a lie, we build a house of cards that will fall to men seeking control and power. History tells us time and time again that to deny what is right and true and embrace what is wrong and false is to fall prey to the rule of the gang or the tyranny of one. We need look no further than Mao, Mussolini, Stalin, Pol Pot, or Robespierre for such evidence.

I am a liberal because I believe in liberty. I believe liberty is the antithesis of slavery and slavery is the unavoidable outcome of lies: lies about who we are as people, lies about what is right and what is wrong, lies about man and lies about God.

Disregard for the objective meaning of words has led us to believe that liberals are those who want less liberty rather than more. Progressives have spun reality and turned it on its head. In their fluid rainbow lexicon, love is now synonymous with sex and hate is now synonymous with love. Men are women and women are men. We have truly come to the point where red is a number and two plus two equals green.

All these lies have led our culture to depart from the values required by a virtuous society. It starts with the little things, like definitions of everyday words. Departure from the established boundaries of the playing field means a departure from the idea of absolute truth. And departure from ascribing true meanings to words has blinded us from any hope of seeing reality for what it truly is. It has placed us in the Matrix, ruled and dominated by whatever leftist brats happen to demand that day. That doesn't bode well for a society that once aspired to good government and virtue.

Made Free by Truth

One of the most important questions you can ask yourself is this: Are we really free today, or are we becoming more and more enslaved by the constructs of the Übermensch—the Superman—the power brokers, the elites, the "fittest" who have survived in the political arenas of campaigns or campuses?

Are we free to live within the boundaries of justice that come from the classical liberal education—of the Uni-Versity, the Uni-Verities, the Uni-Veritas—or are we becoming more and more bound by groupthink, political correctness, and populous power—what M. Scott Peck calls the diabolical human mind?

You see, good education must be grounded in the conservative respect for what is immutable, just, and real. It should seek to reclaim what has been co-opted and to reveal what has been compromised. Good education should be free of intimidation and should honor open inquiry and the right to dissent. It should have confidence in the measuring rod of truth—that unalienable standard that is bigger and better than the crowd or the consensus.

Education—good, liberal education—teaches young men and women the art of pursuing truth, not constructing opinions. As Martin Luther King Jr. told us in his letter from Birmingham Jail, good education aims to conserve the immutable virtues that serve as our strongest justification for our ongoing struggle for freedom, liberation, and liberty. I am not sure anyone can truly call himself a liberal if he doesn't share these basic conservative ideas.

It seems that hardly a day goes by when the call for "safe spaces" and "speech codes" is not headline news. These countless stories show that colleges and universities today are more bastions of ideological fascism than bulwarks of free speech, places where students and faculty alike are more passionate about restricting debate than they are about defending the freedom to disagree.

Perhaps a refresher in educational history would help all of us. We might do well to remember the academy's rich heritage in the liberal arts and its millennia-old commitment to freedom of speech, freedom of expression, freedom of inquiry, and freedom of thought. We all might be a bit better off if we reflect for a moment on the higher ideals of classical liberalism and human freedom.

The answer to the riots and rebellions we see on our campuses from coast to coast, from Berkeley to Brown and many other college campuses in between, is not found in the tyranny of false "tolerance" or the ideological safety of "trigger warnings." It isn't found in more restrictions and more legalism. It isn't found in perpetuating victimization, violence, or vengeance. It is found in returning to the age-old mission of the liberal arts academy: in *veritas*, in the pursuit of truth and the practice of wisdom, in being men and women of virtue, not vice. Remember what C. S. Lewis told us in *The Chronicles of Narnia*: the answer is always found in what is good, not in what is safe.

Human freedom, intellectual or otherwise, was not born in Berkeley, but rather in a community called Bethlehem some two thousand years ago. The fundamental principles of higher education are grounded in the Word, that Truth that was made flesh and dwelled among us. It is founded in the Logos, the eternal preexistent "alphabet": the alpha and the omega, the beginning and the end, the *creatio ex nihilo*.

The freedom our nation's schools claim to hold so dear finds its home not at a campus near the sandy beaches of our West Coast, but rather in a stable under the stars in ancient Israel. Free speech (at Berkeley or anywhere else for that matter) has never been achieved outside of the context of the foundational admonition—dare I say biblical admonition—stated very succinctly in Berkeley's own founding motto: "*Fiat Lux*," "Let there be Light."

Anyone who is serious about learning, whether they be teacher or student, ought to be guided by the implied objectivity of that "Light"— by the immutable and not the malleable; by the right, the just, and the true, not by the transient constructs of tolerance, trigger warnings, safe spaces, microaggressions, and whatever happens to be politically correct on a given day. As Os Guinness said: "All truth is true even if no one believes it, and all falsehood is false even if everyone believes it. Truth is true and that's just the end of it."

The goal of the university, whether it be Berkeley or Baylor, should be what is factual and not the newest fluid fad. Honesty demands that we boldly pursue ideas tested by time, defended by reason, validated by experience, and confirmed by revelation. We will only find truth when we place our confidence in it and not in ourselves. We only learn when we love truth enough to measure all ideas with a measuring rod outside of those things being measured and are willing to discard those ideas we find to be intolerable, inferior, and useless.

History has taught us time and again that political power always raises its angry fist when timeless principles are lost. We know that without the scale of "self-evident truths" grounded in the "laws of nature and nature's God," every culture eventually finds itself subject to the rule of the gang or the tyranny of the individual. Recognizing this, scholars and wise men of all ages have confidently given their hearts and minds to the words, "You shall know the truth and the truth shall set you free."

We'd also do well to remember that God laughs at the wisdom of man. Our truths must always be measured against his Truth with a capital *T*. Our wisdom is no better than "his foolishness." As 1 Corinthians 8 says, "We sometimes tend to think we know all we need to know…but sometimes our humble hearts can help us more than our proud minds. We never know enough until we recognize that God alone knows it all."

When we compromise the definition of words and their meanings, we compromise our ability to debate or disagree. We shift from being critical thinkers to little more than parrots for what is popular and in vogue. C. S. Lewis expressed this type of shift as he scolded the agnostic (remember that he was one for the better part of his life) in *The Great Divorce*:

> Our opinions were not honestly come by. We simply found ourselves in contact with a certain current of ideas and plunged into it because it seemed modern and successful…. [Y]ou know, we just started automatically writing the kind of essays that got good marks and saying the kind of things that won applause. When, in our whole lives, did we honestly face, in solitude, the one question on which all turned: whether after all the Supernatural might not in fact occur? When did we put up one moment's real resistance to the loss of our faith?

Freedom is found in truth. Liberty, true intellectual liberty, is often found in conserving the ideas tested by time rather than running mindlessly after the newest fad. Only by submitting to God's Truth, a truth outside of ourselves, are we free from the vicissitudes of men.

Walking on Ice

Life's journey is analogous to crossing a frozen lake at the beginning of spring. Much of the ice is thin, and we know very well that we cannot and should not step on it. The secret to avoiding disaster is to look for the places where the ice is firm and solid.

You have to look for what is thick and avoid what is thin. Or to put it another way, you have to look for what is enduring and stay away from what is melting.

You navigate the lake best by stepping onto the ice that is the same today as it was yesterday. Likewise, we navigate life best by stepping onto those ideas that mean the same thing today that they meant two thousand years ago. It's quite simple. That which hasn't changed in the wake of a floundering culture is the safer bet. Those ideas and beliefs probably haven't changed for a reason. They are still solid and thick because they have been tested over and over again throughout the course of history and have proven firm and reliable.

The principle here is the exact same as previously described in Christ's parable of building on sand or rock. The difference is the foundation. One was solid and one fragile. The solid foundation holds true. The fragile melts and crumbles.

Jesus was very clear: our lives must be built on his enduring truths—on thick ice and hard rock, or as Chesterton once put it, "The point of opening one's mind, akin to that of opening one's mouth, is to close it on something solid."

Whether we call it thin ice or shifting sand, a foundation built on relative truth, moving targets, and fairy-tale definitions will result in collapse and failure. It is the antithesis of maturing and living like an adult. It is perpetual adolescence and juvenile foolishness.

Words have definitions. Meanings aren't changed just because you or I feel like it. Webster has written his dictionary, and you're not Webster.

Love Lost

*"In the end, we will remember not the words of our ene-
mies, but the silence of our friends."*

—Martin Luther King Jr.

If you are honestly following the culture wars in our nation, you must
admit that the ideas and values that once served as the cornerstones of
our constitutional republic are no longer understood, let alone passed
down from one generation to the next as they should be. The key virtues
that once served as the bedrock upon which our free society was built
are no longer even recognized or properly defined.

One of the casualties in this war of ignorance is the virtue of love,
otherwise known as Christian charity. Today it is assumed that love
means tolerance and tolerance means love. But any cursory understanding of these two terms shows that they are not the same, nor do they have
the same moral weight and value. To tolerate someone does not mean
you even care about her, let alone love her. As I once told Bill O'Reilly
when I was on his show, "You didn't send your wife an 'I tolerate you'
card on your anniversary, and there's a reason. It wouldn't have ended
well. Tolerance is an inferior virtue. It says, 'I really don't care, do what
you want. Love, on the other hand, is a superior virtue. It says, 'I care
deeply, enough to tell you to stop.' Tolerance says, 'I couldn't care less.'

Love says 'I care a great deal.' We don't send 'I tolerate you' cards to those we love."

Tolerance, as it is currently practiced, is extended only to those who accept the progressive agenda and fall in line with the approved thoughts, attitudes, and political views of the left. The leaders of the left's movement are so "tolerant" that they feel compelled to dismiss, if not completely shut down, any viewpoints that disagree with their own. Their intolerance for anything that smacks of a traditional viewpoint is on full display as they shamelessly tell Christians and conservative Jews that they are intolerable. They're so tolerant that they protest the likes of Ben Shapiro, Dennis Prager, and Star Parker, as well as those of open-minded secularists like Dave Rubin and Adam Carolla. Tolerance says all are welcome, unless you are Sarah Huckabee Sanders, Candace Owens, or Clarence Thomas.

The tolerance movement has continuously had to redefine itself by endlessly adding to its list of acceptable and unacceptable words and beliefs. There is a constant policing by those in power. Religious freedom is derided. Every day brings new rules and restrictions regarding what you are allowed to think and say. At its core, this movement is about authority and control. Contemporary tolerance has become little more than a thinly veiled experiment, like something out of Huxley's *Brave New World*. Any free thought is a threat to the power of the progressive agenda.

What Is Love?

Thirty-five years ago, Tina Turner topped the Billboard charts by asking, "What's love got to do with it?" When it comes to building a free and virtuous society, the answer is everything.

A truly loving person cares enough to disagree. Love presupposes the freedom of both parties to suggest the other is wrong. It assumes the obligation to stand in the way of someone when he is hurting himself or others and to tell him to stop. Love tries to prevent other people from destroying themselves. It doesn't just tolerate bad behavior. Loving parents refuse to let their children do foolish things. They are intolerant enough to tell their son to stay out of the road. They don't tolerate their daughter putting her hand on a hot stove. The parent who loves her child stands in the kitchen and says "Stop."

Likewise, a true friend tells us when we are wrong. If you are enabling rather than confronting, you might want to do a friendship check. All of us have to be told when we are wrong and that we should stop if we are doing foolish and self-destructive things.

If appeasement is the goal, regret will inevitably be the result. By "tolerating" or showing support for behavior that we know is bad for our friends, we're not doing them any favors. We're not proving our love; we're demonstrating our apathy. We should want the best for those we love, and that means we have to be willing to tell them when we believe that they are doing something that's hurting themselves—whether in body or soul.

Conversely, progressive tolerance demands that we abandon our friends to whatever "moral" code is fashionable at the time. Progressive tolerance is dangerous. It is unstable. It is constantly blown around by the winds of political fads. It is wielded by those who seek power. Radical tolerance refuses to allow for discussion. It has no consistent standard, and its target is always moving. Progressive tolerance refuses to allow anyone to challenge what happens to be popular. Tolerance as it is defined today can quickly become tyranny. It squashes debate, derides dissent, and seeks to control. It silences speech and is anti-freedom.

Progressives strut about in this brave new world naked as a jaybird, wearing their emperor's clothes of "inclusion and acceptance." In these "tolerant" times, those waving their banners of "love" actually look forward to the day of sitting in the Colosseum and being entertained as they watch all who dare dissent from their new orthodoxy being brought to their knees. This world of inclusion is one where those who condemn others for being judgmental yearn for the day when they will judge whom to banish from polite society for thinking for themselves.

The hypocrisy of all of this gets lost on those who have willfully given away one of the greatest freedoms that all humans have, the freedom of thought. Indoctrination has overtaken education as students are being cloned in the spitting image of progressive professors who will tolerate nothing less than full subservience. Welcome to the millennial ivory tower, a place of selfishness, arrogance, and condescension.

Where does change begin? How do we instill in young people the understanding that tolerance is destroying them? How do we teach them what it means to truly love? Where is the hope for future generations?

The change begins when we understand what love is, how it acts, and what it demands. Paul wrote clearly about the nature and characteristics of love in a letter to the Corinthians: "Love is patient, love is kind. It does not envy, it does not boast, it is not proud. It does not dishonor others, it is not self-seeking, it is not easily angered, it keeps no record of wrongs. Love does not delight in evil but rejoices with the truth. It always protects, always trusts, always hopes, always perseveres. Love never fails."[1]

This is the stark contrast between true love and its progressive counterfeit. Patience is not found in rioting against others who disagree. Kindness is not witnessed in ruining the lives of those who think differently. "My feelings are most important" is a declaration of pride and self-importance, neither of which is a characteristic of love.

The stark contrast between love and tolerance is seen in the idea of protection. Love is called always to protect, rather than falling in line with the inferior virtues of tolerance, acceptance, and inclusion. Love is willing to break rank, even when doing so is quite unpopular. Love speaks up when tolerance is silent. True love—that is, Christian charity—sacrifices the self for the sake of protecting others. True love steps in the way and says "Stop." True love cares, while tolerance could not care less.

If love is nothing more than a feeling, it has a shorter shelf life than a loaf of bread. Feelings change. Attitudes are flipped like the quarter before kickoff at a football game. Love is more than the mood we are in on any given day. Love is "for better or for worse, till death do us part." Love loves always, especially when it doesn't feel like it.

Saint Augustine describes it well: "What does love look like? It has the hands to help others. It has the feet to hasten to the poor and needy. It has eyes to see misery and want. It has the ears to hear the sighs and sorrows of men. That is what love looks like." In other words, love is not an affectionate feeling, but a steady wish for another person's ultimate good.

John wrote in his Gospel, "Whoever does not love does not know God, because God is love."[2] Who defines what love is to us? If it is defined by a gang pushing an agenda, then love is lost. But if God is the very definition of love, then we learn what love is by learning more about God.

God is anything but tolerant. He stands against the things that separate us from him and from others. The love of God is more than a feeling that he has for us. It is an unchangeable and eternal fact. God's love is action, the greatest act of which was the Incarnation of Christ. God does not tolerate us! He gave His life for us! "Greater love has no man than this, that a man lay down his life for his friends." This is so much more than mere tolerance. This and this alone is love.

Love is not simply telling people they are right because they want to be told they are right. Love is caring enough for someone, regardless of what foolish things they may say or do, to step in their way and protect them from making bad choices that are, frankly, intolerable.

This is unfailing love, caring and compassionate, unconditional and unrelenting. As Dr. David Jeremiah commented about the assertion in 1 Corinthians 13:8 that love never fails, "Love never fails because God never fails, and God is love."[3]

Brush Your Teeth before Leaving

"To change your life you need to change your priorities."

—John C. Maxwell

In Agreement

While you may disagree with some things I've written so far, I'm sure you can agree with these two basic statements:

First, it's important to brush your teeth.

Second, no one should ever leave home without doing so.

But at a time when colleges across the country are offering counseling centers complete with teddy bears, coloring books, Play-Doh, and videos of frolicking puppies to soothe our nerves and calm our anxieties, perhaps I'm wrong. When you have universities offering "nap times" in their college libraries and baby goats to pet during finals week, maybe a few words on the basics of oral hygiene are warranted. When more college students show up for class wearing their pajamas than a pressed shirt and jacket, maybe I'm not that far out of line to suggest we need to revisit some of the basics of how to effectively function in an adult world. Sorry if this threatens anyone's sense of safety, but one of the first things we might want to consider doing each and every morning before we head to work or run off to class is brushing our teeth. It is a good thing to do.

Certainly we can all agree that we need to be teeth-brushing people.

All of the lessons in this book are important. Hopefully they are all grounded in some measure of wisdom that, if followed, will result in us leading more enjoyable, integrity-filled, and successful lives. I believe much of what I have shared to be important concepts by which some of our world's most noble and successful people have stood throughout the course of history. Following these lessons was essential to the leaders in the march for human dignity and human freedom. But I would be remiss if I provided a list of the most important things we should do in order to accomplish our goals, succeed in our careers, have successful marriages, and become effective parents if I didn't first remind you to attend to the basics. Priorities matter. If you get the answers to the basics wrong, then everything else thereafter will crumble.

The old axiom "Don't put the cart before the horse" has been around awhile for a reason. It expresses a basic principle of life that has been proven over and over again from generation to generation: first things first. A man who gets his priorities straight is a man who will get the other stuff right, too.

What Matters Most

For me, the top of the list of what matters most begins with my trust in Jesus Christ. My standing with God is the most important aspect of my life. It is my *summum bonum*, my "highest good." This drives every other decision I make in life. It is the first thing I attend to each morning and the last thing I think about every night. It serves as the pretext and foundation for every decision I make, every thought I have, and every word I speak. It drives me to my knees in prayer. It raises me to my feet in praise. It breaks me in confession. It pushes me to excel. It renews my spirit. It cleanses my heart. Not only does it inspire me to pursue greatness, but it relieves me of my guilt. It is a necessary hygiene of my soul and mind.

The number one priority in my life is that I die daily to myself and become a new creation in my Savior. Being a Christian means being transformed. My identity is in my Lord, not my libido. I am born again, not born that way. Living this out is done in spiritual disciplines—prayer, confession, Bible reading, Bible study, church attendance, service to God, evangelism, pursuit of righteousness, practicing wisdom, and the list goes on.

I have made a commitment to God, and through living out that commitment I have found that following Christ is not just the best way to die, but the best way to live. This is true not just for me personally, but also for my family and friends around me, for thanks to my desire to be to be Christ-like, to be a Christian, I am much easier to live with than I would ever be if I tried to live without him. All of this isn't just something that happens haphazardly—it is the result of actively and intentionally carrying out these disciplines and practices each day.

Faith is vitally important, and it cannot be maintained without work. Yes, it is very true that "it is by grace that we are saved through faith, it is not of our own doing. It is a gift of God, not of works, lest any of us should boast." But Jesus himself also said, "If you love me you will obey me." Like anything else in life, faith is strengthened through routine, hard work, commitment, and priorities.

So, what does a daily regimen of spiritual hygiene look like? What does it look like to work out your faith with fear and trembling?

Well, first we must understand that faith is not just a lazy acquiescence to the existence of God, but rather an active and engaged, routine and rigorous relationship with God. It is a marriage with Christ, and like anyone who has been married to the same spouse for twenty or thirty years will tell you, marriage is an act of the will; it is hard work.

Faith is active. It is not passive. Faith is integrated, not segregated. Faith integrates head and heart, reason and emotion, and belief and behavior. Faith practices what it preaches.

We are only given so much time, so much energy, and so many resources in a given day. We have to budget our efforts and invest wisely so that we can then spend what limited time, energy, money, and talent we have on what we value the most.

The same is true with faith. The faith we've been given by God's prevenient grace needs to be invested well if it is to grow and strengthen. Hiding it in a hole in the backyard does no one any good. My friends who need it will never see it. And I don't even benefit from it if it is hidden. An "uninvested" faith, tucked away where it doesn't even earn some interest, is of no use.

Every one of us looks back at some of the decisions we have made with money and wishes we had made better choices. Yet frivolous spending or other boneheaded moves can be redeemed and corrected. Student loans can be paid off, credit cards can be cut up, cars can be sold, and overdue bills can be paid. But in real life, the currency that matters most—our time—cannot be redeemed. Every day lost in faithless living is spent and gone. We can't borrow more. Each of us is given only so much of it. As the Bible tells us, our days are numbered.

We all seem to get the concept of budgeting money; we plan the amount we're going to spend and what we're going to spend it on. We do this so that we can pay what has to be paid and/or buy what we want most.

Let's dial it back to our childhood. Likely there was something you wanted to buy. Maybe it was a Red Ryder BB gun like Ralphie dreamed of owning in the Christmas classic *The Christmas Story*. Maybe it was your first Xbox, your first pair of Air Jordans, or your first car.

Whatever it was, you likely needed to set your priorities by doing things like getting a job, doing your chores, or whatever it was as you saved up for the big purchase. You knew there was a certain amount of money you needed to buy exactly what you wanted. You also knew that if you decided to spend your money on candy or junk toys at a dollar store, you'd not reach your goal.

The same principle is true with time.

Stephen Covey is seen by many as a guru of how to live an effective and productive life. In his book *The 7 Habits of Highly Effective People*, he simply said, "Schedule your priorities."

My number one priority is my faith. My close second is my family. I therefore schedule my time accordingly. I invest in these priorities. Doing so grows them and makes them stronger. Not scheduling time for them diminishes and weakens them.

I have other priorities too. For example, I wanted to write this book. If I didn't schedule the time needed to do so, it wouldn't have been written. I do my share of speaking and writing articles. If I don't schedule time for these priorities, they don't get done. As a university president I had many goals and objectives. Time was limited, so scheduling priorities was the only way to stay on task. Not doing so would have resulted in a failed rather than successful presidency.

But there are other items on my list of what I find important. Friends and other family members. Staying in shape and my personal health. Building an adequate retirement account. Mission and charity work. Political activities. All of these things are important to me, and all of them are on a graduated scale of priorities.

You have your own list, and some of the items on it are probably similar to mine. But whatever your priorities are, it is a simple principle of successful living that we all must set priorities in both the complex and mundane things of life if we are ever going to meaningfully engage the culture or have any hope of leaving a positive mark on the world.

The things that you value the most should set the schedule for your daily life. If they don't, then you don't really value them.

First Things

In "God in the Dock," C. S. Lewis referred to first things and second things. He wasn't just speaking of the top of his priority list. Rather, the first things for Lewis were the more meaningful aspects of life—trust in God and obedience in following him at the top. He wrote, "Put first things first and second things are thrown in. Put second things first and you lose both first and second things."

In talking about these first and second things, Lewis borrows from Jesus. Saint Matthew quotes Christ this way: "But seek first his kingdom and his righteousness, and all these things will be given to you as well."[1] The message of Jesus is that if we make his way, his truth, and his life our top priority—our first thing—then the rest of life, the second things, will fall in place and "be given to us as well." Context expands on this truth even more. Preceding the verse just quoted is a passage of the Bible about "storing treasures in Heaven." Lewis, as well as Jesus, is saying that when we live for the eternal rather than the temporal—that is, when we store up treasures in heaven—we get not just the reward of the eternal life to come, but we also enjoy the best of the temporal life too. In other words, place all the secondary things in life in the context of what is first and you get not only the first but also the second to boot. But reverse the order and it all comes crumbling down. Again, priorities matter!

The teachings on "storing up treasures" and "seeking first" are connected. This context implies that when we seek God and his ways first, then true treasures follow.

Now, it is very clear that Christ is not diminishing our temporal needs. Many of his miracles are examples of him providing them. He feeds people, turns water into wine, heals the blind and the lame, and so on. He is not telling us to ignore these needs. What he is telling us is to put them in the proper perspective. He is speaking to the priorities. He is telling us, "What good is it for a man to gain the whole world but lose his soul?" First things first! "For whoever will save his life will lose it, but whoever loses his life, for my sake, will find it." The path to God's provision is to focus on the things that really matter rather than the things that really don't. First things will bring the second. Second things never lead us to those that are first.

Our lives consist of certain ambitions, dreams, and goals. In preparing for a career, we hope that we can work to provide our basic needs and accomplish those dreams. We want to build our homes, provide for our families, and hopefully make a difference in the world. The path for accomplishing all of this is summed up best by this simple axiom: seek first his kingdom and his righteousness and all these things will be added unto you.

Putting God first realizes these good things in an orderly way; reversing the order always leads to disorder, dysfunction, and chaos.

When we live merely pragmatic and materialistic lives, apart from eternal ideals and values, our foundation is weak. It will not sustain us. The more weight that life brings to bear on this foundation, the more likely it is to fail. As the burdens of career, marriage, kids, and family increase, the more likely it is that this weak foundation will fall apart.

Each of us needs to be a person of substance, not just a person of sustenance. Some have said that our priorities are a reflection of our character. If this is so, it might be wise for us to stop and ask: If I have no clear priorities, is it possible that my character is unclear too?

If I learned anything from being a university president for the past decade and a half, it is this principle of first things and priorities. Education should be about promoting unity, not division. It's called a "university" and not a "di-versity" for a reason. Classical education—truly liberating education—should champion the common cause of personal righteousness, not the self-righteousness of our personal whims and fancies. Prioritizing second things always results in exclusion rather than inclusion, segregation rather than integration. Second things always divide; they never unite.

And it's not enough simply to list our first priorities—our actions toward them truly show what our priorities are. Mahatma Gandhi famously said, "Action expresses priorities."

Jell-O Doesn't Nail to the Wall

"Opinions are preferences amid options. Convictions are woven into one's conscience."

—Ravi Zacharias

Knowing how to compromise is an important skill in life.
    When it comes to whose family you will spend the holidays with, compromise is a strength. The color of the walls in the house is a topic on which compromise can be reached without much bloodshed. Compromising on a Friday evening movie choice is perfectly acceptable.

In all these circumstances, compromise allows us to resolve conflict and come to agreements with our friends and family. It's an essential component of human relationships and something we ought to encourage.

There are other times, however, when compromise is unacceptable. Knowing the difference between times to compromise and times to be steadfast is part of being an adult. When convictions, morals, standards, and truth are involved, there is no room for compromise.

Not today.

Not ever.

Country Song Says It All

A host of jokes are made about country songs. Play the song backwards and you get your dog back, your job back, and your girlfriend back. However, a country song that was released in the early 1990s has a message that is desperately needed today.

Aaron Tippin's song "You've Got to Stand for Something" reached number six on the country charts in 1991. The song was an anthem about being true to yourself, standing for what you believe in, and never wavering. The chorus explained that if you don't stand for something, you will fall for anything. Over the course of the hot, long summer of 1991, the reminder of having conviction filled the airways, imploring listeners to stand up for something in life.

Tippin's song became a theme song for those fighting in the Gulf War. His USO tour with Bob Hope helped cement the song's place in history. Taking on deeper meaning for the troops, the song reinforced the need to fight for something in life and to choose the right things to fight for.

Where do we stand in life? What is it that we believe in deeply enough to remain standing regardless of the consequences?

G. K. Chesterton said, "Impartiality is a pompous name for indifference, which is an elegant name for ignorance."[1]

Impartiality is the same as saying "I don't care." It lacks conviction and screams compromise. In the summer of 2019, pastor and bestselling author Joshua Harris caused a controversy when he publicly recanted all he had previously written, turned his back on the God he had proclaimed for years, and walked away from his faith and his family. In an Instagram post, of all places, Harris shared, "The information that was left out of our announcement is that I have undergone a massive shift in regard to my faith in Jesus. The popular phrase for this is 'deconstruction,' the biblical phrase is 'falling away.' By all the measurements I have for defining a Christian, I am not a Christian."[2]

What had been the defining commitment of his life for twenty years was compromised in one social media post.

Many Christians reacted by throwing stones, which is not my intent. My point, rather, in bringing this up is to highlight that what Harris did is indicative of a growing and disturbing trend.

Why couldn't Joshua Harris just walk away silently?

Why did he have to make compromising his faith and his marriage a spectacle for the world to see?

Sure, he mentioned reasons for recanting the words he had written in his book, such as feeling that those words were no longer true to what he believed. He apologized to the LGBTQ folks he said he had hurt and apologized for a myriad of other conservative stances he had held for so long.

But why did it have to be a big show?

Appealing to a new audience (and perhaps addicted to fame?), it appears Harris could not stop himself from making a spectacle of something that would seem to be a bit embarrassing, to say the least.

He could have walked away from his faith in silence without saying a word. Doing so privately would not have changed the fact that he walked away, but it would have garnered far fewer headlines and affected far fewer people.

But instead he had to shout it from the rooftops.

He had to let it be known to all the people of the world that he, Joshua Harris, the bestselling author, the megachurch pastor, the superhero for the faith, had turned his back on the Christ he had claimed to serve. He was now a champion of things he had once stood against. His proclamation revealed more than a change in thoughts and beliefs. It revealed a person whose thoughts and beliefs, as well as motivations, should be questioned.

Can a man be trusted if he gains fame and notoriety because of his commitment and then walks away from that commitment to immediately begin championing an antithetical worldview? If he was willing to turn his back on everything that he said was so important before, why would you believe he won't someday do the same regarding all that he says is so important now? When will the next compromise come?

People change all the time. They change hairstyles, hobbies, musical tastes, and diets. We change clothing. We change addresses. However, at some point, hopefully sooner rather than later, we all grow up and make some decisions as to who we are, what we really believe, and what we will never change.

And quite frankly, it doesn't need to be headline news. The way we live our lives makes this clear for all the world to see. We don't need to call a press conference or take to Instagram.

If you stand for nothing, you will fall for anything. You will flip and flop your way from job to job, church to church, team to team, and marriage to marriage. Impartiality means you are ready to sell your soul to the highest bidder or newest fad at any given moment. When difficulty comes or pleasure beckons, you will compromise.

Paul wrote to the Galatians, "Am I now trying to win the approval of human beings, or of God? Or am I still trying to please people? If I were still trying to please people, I would not be a servant of Christ."[3] His conviction had altered the entire course of his life. These weren't just words on Twitter or Facebook. This was his life. It was his character. It was his identity, and it was not fluid. It was fixed. It was his very soul.

People like Joshua Harris don't inspire confidence. Even though we may want to give the benefit of the doubt, we intuitively recognize their hypocrisy and selfishness. We see no conviction, no consistency, and no integrity, and we rightly think: If he wasn't telling me the truth before, then why would he tell me the truth now? It's the age-old suspicion that the guy who cheated on his first wife will most likely do the same with his second. Where there is compromise there is no trust.

Politics is rife with this form of compromise. Every day we listen to promises that we know the candidate has no intention of keeping. There is a reason no one trusts Congress, and that reason is called compromise.

In April 2019, the Pew Research Center released results from a poll confirming that Americans have a deep distrust for government. According to the release, "Currently, 19% of Millennials (now ages 23–38) report trusting the government, similar to the shares of older generations who say the same. Trust in the government remains at or near historically low levels across generational lines."[4]

The root cause of these terrible numbers is obvious: it's called lying. An overwhelming majority of people believe politicians will do anything simply to get elected. Their words mean nothing. We assume there is zero conviction and zero commitment. And more often than not, we are proven right. When you are known for all your compromises and no one can think of one thing that you actually stand for, guess what? I don't trust you.

Sad as it is, we have come to expect this of politicians. But where it is most disappointing and even more damaging to our cultural DNA is when it is found in the church and in Christian leaders.

A poster-child example of this is the story of the California Assembly Concurrent Resolution 99 (ACR 99). This was and is a resolution that called for Christian "counselors, pastors, religious workers, educators," and all others "with great moral influence" to stop saying anything negative about homosexual and transsexual behavior. The resolution was brought forward to the floor of the California State Assembly for testimony and comment. Kevin Mannoia, the chaplain at Azusa Pacific University (a Christian liberal arts university in Southern California) and the past president of the National Association of Evangelicals, made news by publicly supporting the resolution. His stance on the issue showed a complete lack of conviction and a willingness to equivocate on a worldview he had promised to defend for his entire professional life. His decision to speak in favor of throwing his fellow Christians under the bus simply for standing firm in their biblical convictions screamed of an absence of moral character. It shouted compromise.

Mannoia and I share similar backgrounds in the Wesleyan/Methodist tradition. Our religious roots run deep into the same ecclesiastical soil. It is in the context of our shared tradition, which we internally call the "holiness movement," that Mannoia rushed to engage in what was, by all appearances, little more than soulless pandering.

A little history might be appropriate here.

The entire Wesleyan/Methodist movement was born out of one of the most politically contentious issues in our nation's history. It was called slavery! In fact, during the Civil War, the founders of the Wesleyan Church specifically challenged the Methodist Episcopal Church (our parent church) for not taking a stand against the buying and selling of other human beings as little more than chattel. Two men named Orange Scott and Luther Lee stepped forward and simply said that this was unbiblical and wrong. When it came to the dignity and identity of all human beings, the biblical imperative of human freedom, and the defense of all human life, Scott and Lee would not compromise. They were basically driving a stake in the ground on the basis of two things: first, the teaching of the Bible, and second, the teaching of the founder of Methodism himself, John Wesley.

Wesley was a man of action, not just words. He believed in the "methods of holy living." To paraphrase him in today's parlance, Wesley's message to the Church of England and the broader Christian community was basically this: "You may still have orthodoxy, but you no longer have orthopraxy. You are not practicing what you preach." He condemned the hypocrisy of separating belief from behavior. He called the church to obedience and constantly reminded the people that their identity was in Christ, not in their desires or passions.

Wesley knew that the church would only succeed if it had the courage to stand firm. He knew that we must run into the storm and not away from it. We must wave the banner of scriptural truth and have confidence that if we win waving that banner, it's through God's grace, but if we lose, then that's of secondary importance. The battle is paramount, and we must be willing to go down fighting. Selling our souls for the sake of government approval dishonors our mission, our message, and our very reason to exist. If we become nothing but pale copies of the world around us, then why in the world would anyone want to buy what we are selling?

Wesley understood that compromise always leads to our demise. We will be "thrown out and trampled underfoot" by a culture that laughs at our irrelevance. We are supposed to preserve culture, not take part in its rot. We are supposed to shine a light on evil, not have a conversation about it. We are supposed to confront sin, not capitulate to it.

Wesley understood from history as well as his own experience that compromise never leads to salvation. He knew only too well that you can never bend a knee to the rage mob. Never. Recanting didn't save Cranmer from the fire. In the end, he still burned.

Be Willing to Be True to Yourself

One of the greatest examples of conviction comes from the Old Testament prophet Joshua. As he stood before the Israelites, Joshua wasn't sure what the people would do. If the best predictor of future behavior is always past behavior, Joshua understood there was only a slim chance that the children of Israel would choose God and forsake all the rest.

Despite the odds not stacking in his favor, Joshua refused to compromise. He stood in front of the crowd and called on the people to make a choice. He challenged the nation: "Now fear the Lord and serve him with all faithfulness. Throw away the gods your ancestors worshiped beyond the Euphrates River and in Egypt and serve the Lord. But if serving the Lord seems undesirable to you, then choose for yourselves this day whom you will serve, whether the gods your ancestors served beyond the Euphrates, or the gods of the Amorites, in whose land you are living."[5]

He called for conviction among God's chosen people. He demanded that they stand for something without compromising, that they be steadfast and immovable.

But Joshua did not put it simply on the people. He knew that he, too, had to make a stand. He had to lead. He was obligated to set an example, to talk the talk and walk the walk. He had to be willing to practice what he preached. To practice "the methods" of holy living, he had to be a man of integrity, character, and purpose.

So rather than stopping with the challenge, Joshua revealed his character. He showed his conviction by taking a stand for his God. "But as for me and my household, we will serve the Lord," he bellowed.

Joshua didn't wait to see what others were doing or what they would choose. He didn't allow his decisions to be influenced by the whims of his peers or the whispers of politicians. He spoke with the courage, clarity, and conviction the nation needed. Come hell or high water, he was dedicated to the Lord. He had made that his commitment.

This is the leadership required of all of us. Our kids need to see it. Our students need to see it too. Our culture and our world are begging for it. Leaders lead. They are committed. They have conviction. They don't compromise.

Make a commitment to that one thing that you will never compromise. Find the conviction to be steadfast and immovable. Stop equivocating and have the courage to march forward in the face of adversity. Give people the confidence that you will never turn back, and you will be amazed how many will gladly follow.

Conviction and commitment set true leaders apart from the multitude. No one is going to follow someone who is going to sell his soul to the California State Assembly or sell out his faith and his wife on social media.

Paul wrote, "Therefore, my dear brothers and sisters, stand firm. Let nothing move you. Always give yourselves fully to the work of the Lord, because you know that your labor in the Lord is not in vain."[6]

This is leadership.

Stand for something.

When people look at you, let them know they need never second-guess who you are, where you are going, or what you represent.

Grown-ups don't change their minds with each passing political fad. Leaders don't reverse course just because they feel like it.

Franklin Graham wrote in the March 2019 issue of *Decision Magazine*, "With God's help, we will pray, we will stand boldly for God's truth, and we will never compromise with a godless culture that defies and despises the principles of Scripture."[7]

The faithful realize that there is no reason to look back and there is never a reason to stop fighting for what is right. The fight for justice, for truth, and for righteousness is not a battle that will end anytime soon. Failing to enter the battle, failing to stand firm, failing to lead with unremitting conviction and courage is what children do. It is adolescents who choose popularity over principle. This is not the behavior of an adult.

A person who has no set standards takes to beliefs and opinions like Jell-O being nailed to the wall. The convictions he professes will never stick. Such a person is a "child who is tossed and blown about by every wind of new teaching [and] influenced by people who try to trick us with lies so clever they sound like the truth" (Ephesians 4:14).

An adult is one who not only lives for more than the winds of popularity, but does so with purpose and uncompromised passion.

In the early 1900s, the Indian Christian Sadhu Sundar Singh wrote the first version of the now famous hymn "I Have Decided to Follow Jesus." It is based on the last words of Nokseng, a fellow Christian who refused to renounce his faith in spite of watching his two children and his wife be martyred by a Garo tribal chief. His refusal to compromise is said to have resulted in the conversion of not only the murderous chief, but also many others in a region of India that was, at the time, known for great brutality. History tells us that Nokseng, after watching his own family be killed, responded to the chief's threats that he too would be next if he didn't recant by singing these words: "I have decided to follow Jesus... No turning back, No turning back. Though no one joins me, still I will follow... No turning back, No turning back. The world behind me, the cross before me... No turning back, No turning back."

This song starts with a decision and then speaks of remaining true to the decision regardless of adversity. It is a song of conviction. It is a proclamation of no compromise. Nokseng decided, and there was no turning back.

All of us need to answer the question, "What am I going to stand for in this life?"

Do you want your legacy to be that of Joshua Harris or the prophet Joshua?

Do you want to stand with the likes of Kevin Mannoia or Nokseng?

Leaders make a decision and don't turn back.

They don't compromise.

They sing, "No turning back."

They shout, "Here I stand, I can do no other."

You can nail ninety-five theses to a wall and change the world.

You can't nail Jell-O to much of anything.

Bring Your Umbrella

"As Elisabeth Elliot points out, not even dying a martyr's death is classified as extraordinary obedience when you are following a Savior who died on a cross."

—David Platt

Praying for Rain

Once upon a time, there was a rural community in the Midwest that relied on farming. It had been a rough year, and they were suffering a severe drought. In desperation, the pastors in town got together and called for a community-wide prayer service. It was held at the town's community park, and the whole town came out. Everyone gathered together to pray for rain.

But there was one person in the crowd of a couple hundred people who stood out from all the others. He was the only man that came with an umbrella. In fact, he walked into the prayer circle not only carrying an umbrella, but also wearing a raincoat and boots.

As the man stood next to a few good friends, they looked at him puzzled and asked, "What's up with all the rain gear. Don't you know we're in the middle of a drought?"

The man answered: "True. We are in a drought, but isn't the point of this meeting to ask God to change it? I believe he is listening to us. I believe he will do something about it. In fact, isn't that why we're all here?"

Silence from his friends.

It was clear who had faith and who didn't.

Two hundred came to pray for rain, but only one actually believed the rain would come. Two hundred claimed to be believers, but only one truly was. One came wearing a raincoat and boots and carrying an umbrella. Two hundred didn't think they needed to.

James tells us in his New Testament epistle, "Do you not know, O foolish man, that faith without works is dead." Jesus told us that "if you love me, you will obey my commandments" and, thereby, made it clear that belief and behavior are two sides of the same coin of true faith. Dietrich Bonhoeffer said, "Only he who believes obeys, but only he who obeys believes."

If it is true that actions speak louder than words, the action of having an umbrella in hand while you're praying for rain shouts that you believe in a God who controls the universe, who listens to those who are faithful to him, and who can and does let us participate in his redemptive work through our prayers.

If you claim to believe, then show your belief in your actions. If you claim to be a football player, then go to practice, listen to the coach, memorize the plays, and do the workouts. If you claim to be a musician, then learn the rules of music, rhyme, rhythm, and cadence, and practice.

Memorize the plays, learn to read music, and bring an umbrella. "You say you have faith without works, I will show you my faith by what I do!"

If you're going to be a believer, believe. If you're going to pray, expect God to hear it. If you say you're a follower of Christ, act like it. If you're going to profess to be something, then be the thing you profess. Being a person of faith isn't meant to be just a toe-dipping experience. It is an all-in devotion.

Not a Buffet

Maybe a symptom of much that ails our culture today is all the cheat codes we find in video games. If you have ever played games, or watched your kids do the same, you know that buried in many of these games you can find the right combination of codes that allows you to skip levels, avoid some of the rules, and get a leg up against the game's enemy. The implicit lesson here is that the rules don't matter as much as having the skill it takes to figure out how to break them.

In the old days, games such as Monopoly, Candy Land, and chess came with a little pamphlet that listed and defined the rules. The game was meant to be played by those rules. Breaking the rules had a name: cheating. There were no "cheat codes."

Christianity is similar to the old games, not the new. The rules of Christianity don't change every time someone joins the game. There are no cheat codes that allow you to progress through life with more ease. Doctrine and practice have been established. And the "game" wasn't defined just yesterday. We can trace it back a couple millennia.

Recently, Pete Buttigieg, the former mayor of South Bend, Indiana, and a 2020 presidential candidate, took to the national stage to attack Vice President Mike Pence and, by association, tens of millions of America's orthodox Christians.

"My [homosexual] marriage," said Mr. Buttigieg, "has made me a better man. And yes, Mr. Vice President, it has moved me closer to God. If being gay was a choice, it was a choice that was made far above my pay grade. That's the thing I wish the Mike Pences of the world would understand, that if you have a problem with who I am, your problem is not with me. Your quarrel, sir, is with my creator."

This wasn't an isolated rhetorical cheap shot. Earlier, in 2019, Mr. Buttigieg criticized Vice President Pence by saying, "Who would think that this uber-Evangelical Christian would go down in history as the midwife of the porn star presidency? If he were here you would think he's a nice guy to your face, but he's also just fanatical. How could he allow himself to become the cheerleader of the porn star presidency? Is it that he stopped believing in the scripture when he started believing in Donald Trump?"

Mr. Buttigieg's ridicule of the Pences' religious convictions persists, in spite of the fact that Mr. Pence has done nothing but show grace and respect at every turn. "I hold Mayor Buttigieg in the highest personal regard," said Mr. Pence. "I see him as a dedicated public servant and patriot." There is no record of Mr. Pence's ever insulting Mr. Buttigieg or returning his mockery with similar derision, despite the fact that both served the state of Indiana together when Mike Pence was the state's governor. Mr. Pence has shown remarkable restraint and nothing but civility and a generous spirit of true tolerance.

I won't exercise the same restraint.

While our vice president may find it politically imprudent to respond to such provocations, some of us see less reason to remain circumspect. Presumptuous as it might be to offer a response on behalf of the vice president, I am going to venture a try. Here it goes.

> Mr. Buttigieg, has it ever occurred to you that the "Mike Pences of the world" don't have a problem with "who you are," but disagree with what you do? We believe human identity is much more than the sum of someone's sexual inclinations. In fact, the "creator" whom you so boldly reference makes this pretty clear.
>
> You see, Mr. Mayor, this is a matter of your proclivities, not your personhood. When it comes to your personal peccadillos, the "Mike Pences of the world" really don't want to know. Your sexual appetites are your business. The thing about obedient and faithful Christians is this: we consider someone else's private life to be just that—private. Please stop telling us what kind of sex you like. We don't want to know. If you want us to stay out of your bedroom, please shut the door. Stop opening it up and forcing us to applaud and celebrate.
>
> Oh, I can hear your reply before you even open your mouth, Mr. Buttigieg. It is as predictable as the sunrise. "You're missing the point," you say. "This is not about sex. It is about marriage." Well, aside from the transparent incongruity of this

claim, let's cut to the chase and close with this: What gives you the right to redefine a sacrament of the church? You don't get to make up your own Christianity. You also don't get to make up your own Jesus, and in case you missed it, he is explicitly clear on his definition of marriage: "For this reason a man will leave his father and mother and be united with his wife, and the two will become one flesh."

No, our quarrel really isn't with your creator, sir. Our quarrel is with you.

Do you see what Mr. Buttigieg and so many other Americans have done? They've defined their own Christianity and changed the rules. They think they have found a "cheat code."

Rather than accepting the God-designed plan laid forth by scripture, tradition, reason, and experience, a design supported by two thousand years of Christian history and teaching, they've created a new religion that looks much more like the god they see in the mirror than the one they see in the Bible.

I would love to have this conversation with Mr. Buttigieg himself, but I have had the opportunity to have this same conversation with many students, faculty, parents, and pastors.

Many professed Christians in America share the same soft faith as Mayor Pete—cafeteria Christians who seem to think they can simply pick and choose the parts they like and throw out all the rest.

I once had a friend who shared with me that he hated Subway. Not the subway, but Subway—the sandwich place. His problem? They advertise specialty sandwiches, but when you go to order one of those sandwiches, they still ask you what you'd like on it. When my friend ordered a sandwich, he wanted the one he had seen advertised, not his own creation.

Many Americans think they can treat their Christianity like a Subway sandwich. Instead of buying what's advertised, they can customize the dogmas and beliefs to which they will adhere, even if that results in something wholly unrecognizable from what we have always understood Christianity to mean.

Christian beliefs and practices aren't spread out before us as one grand buffet for our picking and choosing. They're more like the "special of the day" at the local small-town diner. Christianity comes on one plate, as advertised—take it or leave it. You can't make up your own Christianity, much like you can't turn a steak-and-cheese flatbread into a BLT.

Commitment Level

Since we have to take Christianity as it is presented in scripture and has been passed down by the church, not only are the doctrines and practices not up for debate, but neither is the level of commitment. If you're in a group or church that thinks it has the authority to change the time-tested truths of the church—run! Don't run from the faith, but run from that church.

Doctrinal positions aren't meant to be musical chairs. The required level of commitment to those positions and doctrines isn't up for grabs either. Christianity isn't a religion of half measures: it is an all-in proposition. The first shall be last and the last shall be first. He who tries to save his life will lose it. He who is willing to give his life will gain it.

Our culture of political correctness is one that, by definition, seeks to change definitions. Illegal immigrants are called undocumented aliens. Gender-dysphoric men are called women. Neo-Gnosticism is called Christianity. Love is called sex. Sex is called love. Disagreement is called hate. Intolerance is called tolerance. Whining is called woke. Muslim terrorists are called religious extremists.

But does changing any of these definitions change what is true? If a certain sect of Islam is prone to terrorist acts, you can call them extremists all you want—but that doesn't change the reality of the core doctrines they are teaching. You can call an illegal immigrant "undocumented" until the cows come home, but that doesn't make him legal. You can call

Bruce Jenner a woman, but he still has his Y chromosomes. Pretending you have found a "cheat code" to change all these facts doesn't change the actual facts you're dealing with. Claiming the tiger has no stripes doesn't change the fact that he's still a big cat who can kill you.

Again, we don't get to make up our own Christianity. It's not our job to rewrite the definition of the faith. Christianity has a two-thousand-year-old standing definition. Mayors from midsized towns in Indiana don't have any right to redefine it simply because it places some confines on their sex lives. Saint Augustine, who left behind his earthly desires, told us that if you believe what you like in the Gospels and reject what you don't like, it is not the Gospel you believe, but yourself.

Christianity is defined by the Bible, and the Bible teaches us how to be Christian—not Pete Buttigieg, Congress or the courts, you or me. None of us has the prerogative to take the stripes off the tiger.

From the first pages of the scriptures written some 3,500 years ago, we find that Israel was instructed to follow God completely. God promised his chosen people that following his commands would lead them to be blessed and to enjoy the life and liberty God desired for them. But if they refused, they would suffer the consequences of their apostasy. Over and over again, the prophets called the people to remember the blessings of obedience and the curses that come from rebellion. The Book of Kings is just one of the ancient documents telling the story of this sad cycle of promise and punishment.

In the Gospels we find Jesus summarizing (not rewriting or replacing) his laws by telling his followers to love God with all their heart, mind, and soul and to love their neighbors as themselves. He also told them they could not have a divided heart and be his disciples. Matthew even records Jesus teaching his followers to forsake all else: family, career, money, and even concern for life itself in order to follow him.

The epistles of Paul, Peter, James, and Jude continue in the clarity of instruction. In the Book of Revelation, we find all but one of the seven churches in Asia condemned for not following Jesus fully. Believers in

Ephesus, for example, were told to return to their first love. Laodiceans were called lukewarm; they were told that Christ would spit them from his mouth. These are examples of those who weren't completely given over to the faith, who refused to go all in. The rules were made very clear; the definition of the faith was not fuzzy or ambiguous, and there was no "cheat code."

Christianity instructs its followers to be 100 percent committed. There's no just wading in the water. Followers of Jesus are called to dive in and die. And when they surface, they are literally born again, new creations in Christ.

C. S. Lewis told us that "Christianity, if false, is of no importance, and if true, of infinite importance. The only thing it cannot be is moderately important." He also wrote that Christ says to us, "Give me all of you! I don't want so much of your time, so much of your talents and money, and so much of your work. I want all of You! All of You!! I have not come to torment or to frustrate the natural man or woman but to kill it! No half measures will do. I don't want to only prune a branch here and a branch there; rather I want the whole tree out! Hand it over to me, the whole outfit, all of your desires, all of your wants and wishes and dreams. Turn them ALL over to me. Give yourself to me and I will make of you a new self—in my image. Give me yourself and in exchange I will give you Myself. My will shall become your will. My heart shall become your heart."

Go all in, fully believe, and fully commit. You say you have faith, great! Now show your faith by what you do.

If you're going to pray for rain, bring your umbrella.

Be What the Box Says

*"O, what may man within him hide, Though angel
on the outward side!"*

—William Shakespeare

Two Parties

Whatever it is you say you stand for—stand for it. If you don't, then stop saying it.

I have been chastised many times for sounding as if I believe Christians can only vote for candidates on the right. One of these critiques came from a pastor.

In an email outlining my limited knowledge of social psychology as well as my ignorance of cognitive and moral development theories (the focus of both my graduate and doctoral work, by the way), he proceeded to chastise me for what he termed my "confirmation bias."

How was I guilty of such ideological foreclosure?

It seems my sin was my persistent criticism of the ineffectual and bankrupt thinking of "progressives."

"Jesus was neither a Republican nor a Democrat," said my clerical coach. "Your focus on partisan politics only distracts from the message of Christ. Surely, if you were more open-minded, you could find some examples where Democrats are right, and Republicans are wrong?"

Knowing that context is always key, I decided to ask a question or two before succumbing to the temptation of venturing an answer: "Aside from the fact that Jesus obviously was neither a Republican nor a Democrat, because neither party existed at the time, can you tell me what exact political policies are of concern to you? Please be specific," I said.

Failing to get a response, I decided to double down.

"Please show me," I asked, "some specific cases where, as you say, 'Democrats are right, and Republicans are wrong.'

"For example, please provide me some evidence as to why politically correct justice is right, and biblically correct justice is wrong?

"Can you tell me why denying the biological fact of the female is right, while defending the empirical reality of a woman is wrong?

"Why is killing our youngest children right, while fighting to protect them from a political party that's hell-bent on their execution is wrong?

"Please tell me where it is ever right to hide the physical consequences of unbiblical sex, while it's wrong to educate people of its harmful effects.

"Please explain to me why it's right for the state to presume to define marriage (a sacrament of the church), while fighting to keep the government out of the church's business is wrong?

"Please help me understand where the confiscation of private property (that is, stealing it through taxation, debt, and inflation) is right, while defending the right of all citizens to work hard and enjoy the fruits of their labor is wrong?

"Can you provide evidence that ignoring our nation's sovereignty is right, while defending our country's borders (as God told Israel to defend its own) is wrong?

"Please share your evidence proving that indoctrinating our children in schools committed to moral nihilism is right, while 'training up our children in the way they should go' is wrong.

"Please tell me why you think denying God's existence and expunging any mention of him from our courts, our Congress, and our classrooms is right, while honoring him as the author and giver of our unalienable rights of life and liberty is wrong.

"Please show me where dividing our country by race and color is right, while working to unite it by virtue and character is wrong.

"Please provide evidence showing that the constant emphasis on my identity and my victimization is right, while the focus on my responsibility and my obligations is wrong. Please tell me where God ever—ever—blesses and protects a people who deny his existence, boo him at their national conventions, mock his minimal standards of morality, celebrate the killing of his youngest children, debauch five- and ten-year-olds on the altar of sexual politics, and define themselves by behaviors he calls damnable. Please tell me where any of this lunacy is right, and why challenging it as suicidal is wrong."

I didn't get an answer from my pastor friend. In fact, his deafening silence was as dumbfounding as his initial question.

My argument here isn't to tell you what candidate to vote for as much as it is to suggest that if you claim to believe something, then shouldn't your vote be consistent with that belief?

If you claim to believe in freedom, then vote for less government rather than more. If you claim to believe in women's rights, then vote for someone who understands that if women aren't real, they have no rights. If you claim to believe in creation care, then vote for someone who believes in the Creator. If you claim to believe in living water, then your soul shouldn't pour forth poison when pressed.

Pharisees

The Gospels in the Bible—Matthew, Mark, Luke, and John—provide a surprising enemy for Jesus.

The expected enemy of the Jewish Messiah was assumed to be the Romans. They were occupying the land that was his. But Christ didn't treat the Romans like enemies. He showed them compassion.

You might expect the traitors of Israel, such as the Jewish tax collectors who took advantage of their own people, to be Jesus' enemies. But instead he befriended them and even chose one to be part of his inner circle of twelve disciples.

You might think the enemies of Christ would be the "sinners," the murderers, thieves, prostitutes, and adulterers, but there are many recorded accounts of Jesus consoling and even forgiving such people.

No, the scriptures don't paint the picture of any of these people being the enemies of Jesus. The group with which Jesus had the most confrontations was that of the political, academic, and religious elites, the "smarter-than-thou" folks—the Pharisees.

These were the most educated and politically powerful Jews of their day. They were lawyers and teachers. They were akin to a combination of those who walk the halls of our Congress, our mainline churches, and our colleges today.

They were the keepers of the law. They were the law's exemplars. They presumed to tell everyone else which laws they needed and which ones were spurious. They were so serious about this that they kept adding new laws.

They were also the moral authorities. They defined justice. They defined what was good and bad, right and wrong, and true and false. They defined mercy.

Now, at first blush, we might conclude that such upstanding, law-abiding folks would be the first to come to the Messiah's side, and he to theirs. But that's not the case.

In fact, Christ called them "white-washed tombs, wolves, snakes, and vipers." He called them hypocrites. If Jesus had any enemies, it seems to have been them.

Why?

Because they were false. They claimed to be one thing, when in fact they were another. When pressed, their souls poured forth contempt rather than confession, self-righteousness rather than repentance, hypocrisy rather than integrity, and vice rather than virtue.

Jesus named those who didn't practice what they preached dirty cups, whitewashed tombs, hypocrites, wolves in sheep's clothing, snakes, and souls full of death and decay. He lambasted those who pretended to be something they were not, those who lied to themselves and lied to others about themselves. These are the "smarter-than-thou" folks who appeared to be Jesus' only enemies.

But before we are too quick to chime in and say "Go get 'em, Jesus," we might want to take a moment for personal reflection.

Are we really any different? When we are pressed, what pours forth from our soul?

Today, lots of people who claim to be Christians are Pharisees who don't hold any internal conviction. They want the power and authority that comes with interpreting God's word, but they lack the inner feeling and dedication that separates the true believers from the hypocrites. They want to be known as Christians, so they dress themselves in Christian clothing. But inside, they share the same corrupt worldview as so many of their peers.

Practicing what you preach is all-important to any adult who wants to stand for something. Those Pharisees who turn to the scriptures to justify their own aggrandizement rather than fighting for a true faith are guilty of false advertisement (and probably a lot of other sins). They use deceptive packaging to lure in their audience, wrapping worthless gifts in the sayings and teachings of sacred writ.

When squeezed, they reveal their insides. They show that they have a different core than what their outside lets on. That's not leadership—it's cowardice. And if you want to be a good Christian, and moreover a good man, you have to harmonize to the best of your abilities the things you say to the world with the things you do in it.

Don't be a Pharisee; be a Christian.

Listen for Omaha

"My best skill was that I was coachable. I was a sponge and aggressive to learn."

—Michael Jordan

An Audible

Sometimes life needs redirection. There are times when it's clear that if you want success, you have to turn around and take a different route. Often that redirection comes from someone "coaching" us. And evidence shows that those who are coachable find success. Those who are not coachable often run headlong into a brick wall. They're too stubborn to see that what they'd hoped for could've been realized with an ounce of humility and a slight redirection.

Yes, there are times when we need to dig in, stick to the game plan, and resist the urge to bail out on the plan. As discussed earlier, conviction and commitment are better than compromise.

But there are many times when we need to listen for an audible and follow it.

Omaha! Omaha!

Peyton Manning is considered one of the greatest quarterbacks football has ever seen. His storied career includes two Super Bowl wins, one with the Indianapolis Colts and one with the Denver Broncos. Manning was one of the smartest quarterbacks to ever step on the field. He was able to read the defense and know when a set play needed to be changed. He knew when to call an audible.

If you watched football during Manning's career, no doubt you heard him change the play many times. The call was very distinct and clear.

"Omaha! Omaha! Set, hut!"

The ball was snapped, and Plan B was put into action.

Why the change? Why not stick with what he had called in the huddle just seconds before? Why not follow the original plan as called by a coach and offensive coordinator?

The reason is that when his opponents approached the line and set their defense, Manning could see the potential failure of a play before it unfolded. So he changed the plan and called an audible.

Microphones on the sidelines picked up the unique "Omaha! Omaha!" as Manning changed course, turned on a dime, and redirected his team to do something perhaps exactly opposite of what he had just told them to do a couple seconds earlier.

Once, during a postgame interview, Manning explained the "Omaha! Omaha!" call. "It was a trigger word that meant we had changed the play," he said. "There was little time on the clock, and the ball needed to be snapped right now. So, to kind of let my offensive linemen know that 'Hey, we'd gone to Plan B, there's low time on the clock.' It's a rhythmic three-syllable word, 'O-ma-ha, set hut.'"[1]

Manning knew that sticking to the original plan could mean a sack, running a play that went nowhere, or wasting a down. His ability to adjust and change direction gave the rest of his team the tools they needed to succeed, and the call provided fans with a game-time sound that will never be forgotten.

The uniqueness of an audible teaches a very simple lesson: sometimes we need to admit circumstances have changed and, if we are to avoid disaster, scrap the plan, change direction, and run a new play. We need to call Omaha.

There's an old saying that the definition of insanity is doing the same thing over and over again and expecting a different result. The phrase has been attributed to a variety of people, from Albert Einstein to Mark Twain. But regardless of who said it, the truth of the statement is obvious.

Being headstrong and refusing to learn from your mistakes can be a recipe for disaster. Repeating the same old failed play and refusing to learn from your failures only assures that you will fail again. You shouldn't expect different results if you keep doubling down on the same dumb things that led you to fail in the first place.

Life is anything but predictable, and although no one succeeds at anything without being committed to a clear goal and strategy, no plan is fail-proof. Being able to see trouble before it happens and being willing to change course in order to avoid that trouble is a prerequisite for success.

The ancient king of Israel, Solomon, wrote, "There is a way that appears to be right, but in the end, it leads to death."[2]

By all appearances the initial play may seem like the right call.

Your game plan appears spot on.

Victory is so close you can taste it.

But something dangerous has camouflaged itself, and if you don't see it and adjust, you'll head into a trap. You will fail. You will get sacked. And before you know it, you will find yourself in a third-and-long situation where the best you can do is punt.

Is your plan working? Is it leading to the life you want? Or is it possible that the way you've chosen, the one that seemed so right, leads to death rather than life?

The lesson Peyton Manning's flexibility on the field teaches is that all of us should constantly be assessing the state of play. We need to look at the defense and determine what adjustments are necessary. If our game plan isn't working, we need to admit we are wrong, change course, and call an audible.

But there are many times where we don't see everything as clearly as we need to. In spite of all the training and preparation, we just don't see reality for what it is. We are too close to the situation and can't see the whole picture. We are missing something that people further away, those who are on the sidelines, up in the stands, or watching on TV, can see as clear as day. We keep making mistakes and we don't understand why the plan isn't working.

That's when you have to listen to the coach. His job is not only to help you train for the sport and prepare for the game, but also to help you recognize when changes need to be made. The reason he's getting paid is to tell you when to call an audible.

Coaches can often see what the players cannot see. In fact, NFL and college football teams often have coaches perched way up above the field, up in the coaches' box, where they have an aerial view of the entire field of play. They can see everything taking place. They can see the mistakes their players are making. They can see both failures and opportunities that the players cannot see for themselves.

Now, it's obvious that any coach worth his salt wants to win as much as his players do. He wants them to succeed. A coach whose goal was to see his team drop the ball over and over would be a lousy one. Coaches do not intend to lose. Coaches don't want to see their players fail. They are put in a position to get the most out of each and every player, but one thing that drives every coach insane is a player unwilling to be coached.

A person who is unwilling to be coached is so frustrating that he can even cause coaches to give up trying. Mike Tice, the former head coach of the Minnesota Vikings, said as much when he retired. According to the Daily Norseman, "Tice says he's ready to move on from the coaching ranks because 'players today don't want to be coached.'"[3]

Are you coachable in life? Do others want to spend the time with you, to invest in you, or has your attitude pushed them away from you?

Being coachable means admitting you don't know everything. It means recognizing that someone might actually be seeing things you do not see. Being coachable means being willing to go to the sidelines, accept criticism, listen to advice, and change direction.

Being coachable is the opposite of arrogance. It is being humble enough to admit when your plan isn't working and when you need to call another play. Being coachable means arrogance is set aside for the sake of the game and for the sake of the team. Your playing time, your stats, and your ego simply don't matter. Being coachable means listening rather than talking. Being coachable means taking responsibility for your mistakes rather than complaining about someone else's.

Being coachable is necessary to succeed in life, and distinguishes adults from children. We all need to learn from each other in order to grow, even if that means admitting our initial plan was doomed to fail. It can be difficult to trust that someone else wants the best for us, but it's a necessary component of human life. When times get tough, being coachable can make the difference between success and failure, happiness and misery. It can make the difference between life and death.

A Change in Direction

Think about some of the most well-known audibles. History has given us many examples of them.

Harland Sanders worked at a gas station and had other odd jobs in his earlier life. If the name doesn't sound familiar to you, replace "Harland" with "Colonel" and I am sure you will recognize the name. Instead of doubling down on his mistakes, at the age of sixty-two Sanders chose to leave the gas station where he was humbly employed to set out on a new course. If Harland Sanders had not been willing to call an audible, there would be no Kentucky Fried Chicken.

Michael Jordan was at the pinnacle of his career. He already had three championship rings, and from all appearances no one would beat the Bulls in the foreseeable future. In spite of this success, Jordan chose to retire early from the NBA to pursue his boyhood dream of playing baseball. Though Jordan found some success on the diamond, the reason for his fame is certainly not thanks to his batting average. With all the world watching, Michael Jordan was willing to eat crow, change course, and call an audible. He returned to basketball, won three more NBA titles, and concluded his career with six championships in total. He is now believed by many to be the greatest basketball player in NBA history.

Saul of Tarsus was one of the most infamous persecutors of Christians in the earliest days of the church. He had a plan. His strategy was clear. He knew what his next move was going to be and why. He had direction and he was determined. But one day, while he was on his way to Syria to imprison and kill more Christians, he was confronted by an unexpected blitz and sacked by God himself. As he lay on his back in the dust and dirt on the road to Damascus, he heard eternity's coach cry out, "Saul, Saul, why do you persecute me?"

Now Saul could have gotten up, brushed himself off, and doubled down on his goal. He could have convinced himself that the fall from his horse had caused a concussion and caused him to hear voices for a brief moment. He could have arrogantly refuted his friends who were with him and who witnessed the whole thing. He could have ignored his teammates and ignored the coach.

But because he was willing to listen and learn, the world changed.

Because Saul called an audible, we now know him as Paul, the champion of the church and the author of two-thirds of the New Testament. Rather than staying the course to stomp out the church, Paul joined with Peter to become a founder of the church. The enemy of the cross took up his own cross. He repented, reformed, and changed direction. He died to self and became an entirely new creation in Christ. He called an audible.

Ronald Reagan, the fortieth president of the United States, did not make his first mark in politics until later in life. Reagan was a B-list actor and president of the Screen Actors Guild before he left Hollywood behind to run for governor of California. It wasn't until after suffering defeat in his first presidential campaign that he was finally elected as the leader of the free world in 1980, just a few days shy of his seventieth birthday.

Even Reagan's opponents now have to agree that he changed the world through his involvement in politics. If he had remained in Hollywood, content to live the high life of a celebrity, Ronald Reagan would be known for little more than a slew of average movies. Without his willingness to change course, the world would have never heard the iconic words, "Mr. Gorbachev, tear down this wall!"[4] Without Reagan's change of direction, the Iron Curtain might not have been rent in two and the Berlin Wall might not have crumbled. Because of his willingness to call a life audible, Ronald Reagan's words will echo through the halls of human history for centuries to come.

These are all examples of ordinary people who accomplished extraordinary things because they were willing to change. Each one of these people left a legacy that would have been impossible had they chosen to dig in, double down, and force their own initial plan rather than change it.

But each one proved they were willing to be coached. Each was willing to learn something, admit defeat, and forge a new path with a renewed passion and determination.

ACME Approach to Life

An old Warner Bros. cartoon, *The Road Runner Show*, is a perfect illustration of someone who was never willing to call an audible. In each episode, the villain, Wile E. Coyote, tries to catch his prey, the Road Runner, but with each attempt Wile E. Coyote is only able to grasp feathers and failure.

Though he tries to catch the Road Runner over and over with increasingly sophisticated schemes, using anvils, rockets, and even jet-powered roller skates, the coyote never succeeds. The Road Runner always wins. Wile E. Coyote is the picture of failure. He always ends up injured, burned, broken, smashed, and unsuccessful.

But in spite of this, Wile E. Coyote always resorts to the same old thing and the same old plan. He always opens the same box from the Acme Corporation with the same gadgets, bombs, roller skates, silly wings, guns, and ammunition.

But none of it ever works. The coyote never, ever calls an audible.

At some point, we all have to wonder if we are chasing the wrong things. Are our choices working? Are we doing the same thing over and over again and expecting different results, like Wile E. Coyote? Or are we willing to admit our mistakes and change direction, like a Jordan, Sanders, or Reagan? Are we willing to change our names like the apostle Paul?

We all laugh at a cartoon character as he fails over and over again, but it's really not all that funny when we see real people around us living essentially the same way, doing the same stupid things over and over and somehow expecting different results. At some point we all should be willing to ask the Dr. Phil question: "How's that working for you?"

There's a word for banging your head against a wall time and time again—it's called insanity. If something isn't working the way you thought it would, be humble enough to seek advice, listen to the coach, make adjustments, and try again.

Solomon wrote, "For though the righteous falls seven times, they rise again, but the wicked stumble when calamity strikes."[5]

The "righteous" one gets up, calls an audible, and runs the next play. He learns and grows from calamity. He doesn't start whining about "safe spaces" and "microaggressions" and blame everyone else around him for his failure. He doesn't stay in the huddle and expect everyone to give him a big group hug. He accepts his responsibility to call "Omaha, Omaha," and he runs a different play.

A person who is coachable is a person who is transformable. The best athletes realize that their vantage point and their understanding can be limited. They look to their teammates and coaches to help them access the defense they are facing and make adjustments.

The transformable person realizes that "his way" is not as important as the right outcome. He is open to other ways. He learns from his experiences and wants trusted peers to point out his weaknesses. He listens.

All of us are annoyed by the people in our lives who don't listen, people who are constantly interrupting, people who seem to care more about the sound of their own voice than about anything someone else might be trying to say to them.

Paul wrote in his letter to the Romans, "Do not conform to the pattern of this world but be transformed by the renewing of your mind."[6]

Today, many people believe that we should only listen to those who appease and please us, to those who "affirm" us. If anyone challenges us with an idea that we don't like or, heaven forbid, suggests that some of our choices and values might be wrong, we shout them down and silence them.

What does it matter that Ben Shapiro is brilliant and might actually have some good advice to offer? He is a conservative, so he needs to be silenced. He needs to be expelled. We will not listen.

What does it matter that Candace Owens and Star Parker understand the plight of the black community much better than you do? They are conservatives. They should never be invited to speak on your campus. They are verboten.

The list goes on and on.

What does it matter that Dave Rubin used to be part of the radical left and seems to have some exceptional wisdom to share from his experience on *The Young Turks*? What does it matter that David Horowitz used to work closely with the Black Panthers and left them for some very clear and good reasons? What does it matter that Abby Johnson used to be pro-choice and no longer is for reasons that are much more defensible than the worldview she used to hold?

To many, these ideas are too challenging. Instead of listening to competing views, many write off these people as being on the "wrong side of history." But refusing to listen to anyone who disagrees with you guarantees that you will never grow, redirect course, and change. Good luck running into that same brick wall over and over again.

Remember, there is a way that seems right to a man, but its outcome is anything but certain. The outcome of not listening is stagnation, not growth. The outcome of not changing is defeat, not victory. The outcome of talking too much and listening too little, of "doing things that seem right to us" but which others are telling us are simply wrong and won't work, is destruction.

The word transform means "to change in condition, nature, or character."[7] Personal transformation is the opposite of personal destruction.

But transformation often comes from outside of us, from taking the advice of a mentor or coach. Choosing the right coach and listening to the right voice is imperative if we are going to make the right calls and run the right plays in life.

I once heard the story of a tennis player whose high school coach made an impact on him that went well beyond the few years he played tennis in high school. The coach led by example, but the tennis player also knew that the coach loved him and cared for his future. That tennis player went on to play in college, but the results were far different. His college coach cared little about the players and focused on building his resume more than building up his players. The outcomes could not have been more drastically different.

The player had excelled in high school, absorbing all the coach had to teach. His game and skills improved. He took joy in playing the game.

In college, the player began to hate the game. One of the great joys of his life was now a burden. Seeing the college coach for what he was, the tennis player stopped listening, and in the blink of an eye saw his disappointing college career come to an end.

The right coach is imperative. Christ's followers find in him a "coach" that excels above all others. His transformative work takes a heart that once was stone and transplants it with a heart of flesh.

Be the All-Beef Patty

"We make a living by what we get. We make a life by what we give."

—Winston Churchill

Burger Economics

An old Wendy's commercial set out to explain the value of its burgers. In competition with McDonald's and Burger King, as well as other fast food restaurants, Wendy's rolled out an advertisement that took a veiled shot at its competitors. As three older ladies examined a burger, two ladies noted the large and fluffy bun. The third, Clara Peller, gave the burger a more thorough examination.

Upon opening the burger, Peller (as well as viewers of the commercial) sees an enormous bun with a tiny hamburger patty. As she looks for the tiny hamburger patty, she utters the iconic line, "Where's the beef?" The line would be said millions of times after the debut of the commercial in 1984.

The point was clear: what truly makes a burger a burger is the size of the patty, not the bun. After all, the bun is only worth about a quarter. The retail value of a slice of tomato, a slice of onion, and even the piece of lettuce is mere cents. A slice of cheese is also only worth pocket change. So why does a hamburger cost so much in a restaurant? What justifies a cost of five dollars or more?

The actual beef patty justifies the price of a hamburger. A quarter-pound of beef is valued in dollars, not cents, further pointing to the fact that the all-beef hamburger patty is what makes a hamburger a hamburger and why the consumer will pay a few dollars more to consume one.

Of all the ingredients that go into making a burger, the beef has the most value.

What is the most valuable ingredient in a life?

Every life has value, regardless of race, creed, nationality, age, sex, or being born or unborn. Every human being has worth. But what a human being actually does throughout the course of his or her life does not always have value. For instance, the work of Mother Teresa far outweighs the work of a drug dealer. The actions of a nurse are of greater value than that of a Ponzi scheme leader.

The difference between the two is one of moral content and substance. One person's contribution is significant and costly. It has moral depth and weight. It is "meaty," if you will. The other person's is cheap and vacuous. It is void of the "meat" that makes life good. There is no beef.

Doing something of value is important. Sure, it is easier at times to simply do what is comfortable and convenient, but the desire to be of value in your work makes your work more rewarding.

Some people, however, are content to do nothing of value while still thinking they should share in the benefits that only come from living a valuable life.

Bill O'Reilly featured a segment a few years ago where he highlighted the life of a young man, Jason Greenslate, living in California. Desiring to show viewers the abuse of the entitlement system that was taking place, O'Reilly exposed the actions of this young SoCal surfer who refused to work and instead chose to live off the system.

The unmotivated millennial was interviewed by Jesse Watters. By Greenslate's own admission, he had no intention of living any other way. He played in a band, took government handouts, and used food stamps to buy food like sushi and other high-end items. The trouble was that he had no desire to do anything different. Rather than helping those who could not help themselves, he chose to take the handout and do nothing with whatever skills and abilities he had been given. He assumed zero responsibility to live a life of value.

The piece revealed a deep issue that exists in our society today. Many people would rather take a handout than go to work and earn a living. As long as free stuff is being passed around, there is no incentive for the Jason Greenslates of the world to live another way. Sadly, instead of working to take care of themselves and help others, many Americans today simply extend a hand to receive a handout.

Jason Greenslate was an adult. But his behavior and attitude were indicative of a child who had never grown up. He wanted to be taken care of rather than take care of others. His actions and decisions reflected a life of limited value.

Truly mature adults see that being an asset to the community, adding value to organizations of which they are members, and finding ways to contribute to others are ideals worth pursuing. Adults realize that when adulthood begins, so does the expectation that they take care of themselves and others.

Unfortunately, the story of the surfer is becoming more the norm than the exception in our culture. Free college tuition, free cell phones, and free food, open enrollment and open borders. Redistribution is the philosophy of the day—not responsibility.

Rewarding those who have done little to nothing to earn the reward is a cancer that eats at the very soul of a country and culture. When one person sees another getting by without doing anything, selfishness metastasizes and spreads. In the blink of an eye, hundreds of thousands begin to take similar steps in their lives, forsaking hard work for the beach instead of punching a clock and earning a living.

What happened to finding personal worth by making a contribution of substance—a "meaty" contribution—to society? When did the aspiration change from shooting for the stars to aiming for the couch? How is there justification today for excelling in video games rather than excelling in life?

Making a contribution to the world around us should not only be an expectation for an adult, it should also be a genuine desire. Each person has a talent, a gift, an ability, and when used properly those talents help to improve communal life rather than degrade it.

Think for a moment what the world would be like if some of our greatest exemplars had made a decision to sit on their talent and live off handouts. Some of the greatest music would have never been played. Books that have changed the world would have never been written. Advances in medicine that have spared millions from sickness or disease would not have been made if those who helped make those advancements had chosen to binge-watch Netflix their whole life. Children would not learn because teachers would not go to work, choosing to spend their lives looking for a handout rather than giving their students a hand up. Garbage would be piled up in every neighborhood if sanitation workers decided they didn't feel like working.

You see, the abilities you have, no matter how great or how small they may seem to you, are actually for the entire social body. All skills and contributions are needed. "The hand cannot say to the eye, I have no need for you."

There's more to life than binge-watching. Life presents greater challenges than beating a video game. We all have the opportunity and the responsibility to build something that lasts longer than a sandcastle.

Adults see life as fleeting and seek to make the most of the days they are given, leaving behind something of greater value. They see life as a legacy rather than an opportunity for leisure. Whether their contributions are known by millions or only by one, it doesn't matter. What matters is doing something.

So many of today's young people have wasted their talents. They had potential, but lacked the heart to take that potential and turn it into reality.

A pastor once told me how common it is for the terminally ill people he sits alongside to confess their regrets to him. They wish they had spent more time with their family. They regret that they had not taken more initiative. They wish they had done more that truly mattered.

Never do they say they wish they had watched more football games. Never once do they wish they could have watched more reruns of *Friends*. No one ever says they wish they had slept in more on Sunday mornings. No one ever says they wish they had given less money and time to the church.

The bitter despair of wasted opportunities plagues so many deathbed conversations. At the end of life, many recognize that the time they had been given could have been used for something greater. A. W. Tozer famously said, "When you kill time, remember that it has no resurrection." The lifestyle of killing time and neglecting opportunity leads to one place—ultimate regret. Life is a series of moments and opportunities, but once they have passed, there is no chance for the redemption of wasted currency.

Being of Value

You have this life. You have this chance.

Regardless of who you were yesterday, you have the chance to make a mark today, to be of value, to leave an impression that will continue long after you are gone.

A successful life is one that has made the most of opportunity. A successful person is one who uses his talents and abilities in a way that minimizes regrets at the end of life.

It's time to get off the couch. It is time to aim for what is challenging rather than what is comfortable. It is time to give rather than take, and to work rather than relax. Free stuff, like freedom, is never free. Everything comes with a price. Have courage to try; don't sell yourself short. Listen to Teddy Roosevelt, who certainly knew a thing or two about effort: "Courage is not having the strength to go on; it is going on when you don't have the strength. Industry and determination can do anything that genius and advantage can do and many things they cannot."

Pelé, the soccer great, once said, "Success is no accident. It is hard work, perseverance, learning, studying, sacrifice, and most of all, love of what you are doing or learning to do." This truth leads us to the first step of doing what we are created to do in this world.

The first step is to work. You were given the ability to think. You were given the tools required to perform some task to earn a wage. Do so. Rather than waiting for a handout, take matters into your own hands. Get to work. Take a job, any job, and use it to learn and grow and save, with the ultimate goal of making a difference. Stop sitting around and waiting for a CEO position to open up the very first year after you graduate from college.

Pay your dues. Start at the bottom if necessary and work your way up. Do not neglect to see the beauty in earning your keep. Earning your position and your promotion is much more gratifying than being given your position, and any income is better than no income. You may want to start off at the top, but you will not and should not. Put in the hard work, learn the hard lessons, and work your way up. Momentum in employment is the mark of growth. Take care of yourself. Stop expecting others to take care of you.

The second important step is to find a way to give of your time and your abilities. It's not all about you. In fact, very little is about you. It is about who you see out the window rather than who you see in the mirror. One of the greatest rewards you will ever receive is to give of yourself and expect nothing in return. Taking part in church ministries, volunteering for Habitat for Humanity, serving meals at a homeless shelter, or collecting clothes for a clothing drive will give you a perspective of how blessed you are. Giving is a blessing you will never forget. Charles Dickens said, "No one is useless in this world who lightens the burdens of another."

Your job helps you to earn a living. Your volunteerism will help you to gain perspective and give you the chance to impact others. There are people around you every day who need you. You may have failed to see them before, but once you begin looking for them you begin to see the needs that you once overlooked. Be a bell-ringer for the Salvation Army at Christmas. Volunteer to clean up at a homeless shelter. Serve in a soup kitchen. Give away your money, then go earn more so you can give away more. This is the "meat" of life. This is the beef. It's not the bread.

You will not receive a paycheck for doing any of this, but you are making an investment that you will not regret on your deathbed. Remember this admonition from St. Francis of Assisi: "Keep a clear eye toward life's end. Do not forget your purpose and destiny as God's creatures. What you are in His sight is what you are and nothing more. Remember that when you leave this earth, you can take nothing that you have received... but only what you have given; a full heart enriched by honest service, love, sacrifice, and courage."

The third step is to pour into the life of someone else, someone younger than you. The next generation will be impacted by someone or something. As we see in the current climate, most of the influence on millennials and GenZers is coming from the left in the worlds of academia, the media, and the "elite" class in Hollywood. But we also see that nearly all of this influence is misguided, shallow, and counterproductive. It is selfish rather than selfless. It champions entitlement. It focuses on blame and offense. It promotes victimization and vice. If you do the opposite, you will stand out like a sore thumb. You will be countercultural. You will be seen and heard. You will lead, and others will follow.

Be a mentor and strive to mold the next generation. Mentorship is a sacrifice of time, but the wisdom gained by the younger person is needed. No nations that fail to inculcate their foundational principles in their next generation survive. Be a Big Brother or Big Sister. Volunteer as a tutor. Lead a church youth group. Lead young people to be active parts of the world they live in, not passive spectators watching as their lives make no difference. Let them see the joy that comes from mentoring in the hopes that they may do the same for the generation that follows them. Set the standard. Idowu Koyenikan once said, "Show me the heroes that the youth of your country look up to, and I will tell you the future of your country." Be a hero.

To find joy in service is to possess a heart of love.
The heart that gives is the heart that truly lives.

A Yearbook Tells the Story

In any typical yearbook, the senior class pictures feature the involvement of the students during their years in school. They list the sports they played. If a student was a member of the band or in drama, those activities are mentioned. All of the clubs that the school offers are listed, as well as the students who served them.

If you look through those yearbooks, you will see some students with a lengthy list of involvement during their four years at the school. Some served and joined in on nearly everything offered. There are some students, however, who have a vastly different "list" beside their name. If a student took part in basically nothing, their name is listed and followed by a list of one, just the word "student." This often means that they did the least amount of work they could get away with before going back home to sit on the couch and play Pokémon.

The students were all given the same opportunities. Though some may not have had athletic ability, they could have served in the student council. If they had no musical or acting ability, they had the opportunity to be involved with the debate team or the business club. Regardless of who they were, there were countless opportunities to do something and to be a part of the bigger mission.

Some simply chose to do the minimal amount of work and then just go home. They made no lasting difference, no contribution, and no lasting imprint. They were merely known as "student."

If you asked schoolteachers and administrators about the students who were involved with multiple organizations, those students are remembered fondly and their efforts are shown not to have been in vain. They left an impression on the teachers and the administration. However, if you ask them about the ones who chose not to get involved, they struggle even to remember them.

All the students were given a chance. All the students had the same amount of time. All had innumerable opportunities. Some gave up their wants to do something bigger and leave behind a mark. Others did little to nothing.

Jesus shares a parable in the Gospel of Matthew:

> It's also like a man going off on an extended trip. He called his servants together and delegated responsibilities. To one he gave five thousand dollars, to another two thousand, to a third one thousand, depending on their abilities. Then he left. Right off, the first servant went to work and doubled his master's investment. The second did the same. But the man with the single thousand dug a hole and carefully buried his master's money.
>
> After a long absence, the master of those three servants came back and settled up with them. The one given five thousand dollars showed him how he had doubled his investment. His master commended him: "Good work! You did your job well. From now on be my partner."
>
> The servant with the two thousand showed how he also had doubled his master's investment. His master commended him: "Good work! You did your job well. From now on be my partner."
>
> The servant given one thousand said, "Master, I know you have high standards and hate careless ways, that you demand the best and make no allowances for error. I was afraid I might disappoint you, so I found a good hiding place and secured your money. Here it is, safe and sound down to the last cent."
>
> The master was furious. "That's a terrible way to live! It's criminal to live cautiously like that! If you knew I was after the best, why did you do less than the least? The least you could have done would have been to invest the sum with the bankers, where at least I would have gotten a little interest.

"Take the thousand and give it to the one who risked the most. And get rid of this 'play-it-safe' who won't go out on a limb. Throw him out into utter darkness."

Moral of Christ's message? One day all of us will be asked if we invested ourselves in meat or in bread.

At the end of days, we will all be asked, "Where's the beef?"

Wish Everyone a Merry Christmas

"We're saying 'Merry Christmas' again."

—Donald Trump

War of Words

Throughout this book I have continually alluded to the war on words. Or maybe better put, the left's all-out assault on freedom of thought and expression. The battle lines in this vocabulary war shift with each passing day. Over the past decade, we've seen attacks on long-standing definitions as well as on some age-old assumptions of what it means to have freedom of expression and intellectual integrity.

One of the first PC vocabulary skirmishes concerned how to refer to people who had entered the United States illegally. We have changed the word used to describe such people from "aliens" to "immigrants," and now to "undocumented." Proponents of each new label declare the nomenclature that preceded it to be bigoted, xenophobic, and intolerant. Then there came the attack on mascots for college and professional sports teams, with cries of racism, trigger warnings, and victimization. Finally, numerous colleges and universities across the land have issued lists of acceptable and unacceptable words and expressions for their campuses.

One of the most egregious examples of modern-day thought police is found at the University of North Carolina, which, just a handful of years ago, issued a list of words and phrases that it considered "micro-aggressions" and which therefore should not be permitted on the Tar Heel's campus.

This list caught the attention of Fox News's Jesse Watters, who embarked on a journey to UNC to do an investigative report for his "Watters' World" segment on *The O'Reilly Factor*. The list was also reported by The Blaze.

What words and phrases were deemed so offensive that they should never pass the lips of the young learners at this fine university? Here are a few:

You should never say, "When I look at you, I don't see color." It's racist.

Never tell a female "I love your shoes." It's misogynistic.

"Interrupting a female-identified colleague" is always verboten. It's evidence of male toxicity.

"Having an office dress code that applies to men and women differently" is transphobic.

Never suggest that "we should have a staff retreat at the country club."

Never ask a colleague to join you to "play a round of golf." It's evidence of white privilege.

Now, for anyone who has an ounce of common sense, this list is beyond ridiculous. Inviting someone to play golf—a microaggression? Why, yes, for it could make the other person feel lesser if he doesn't have enough money to play golf. Or he may have grown up in a family or situation where he never learned how to play. Or he may just not be any good at the game. Whatever the case may be, you should never invite someone to play such a "privileged" game with you, because you run the risk of putting him in a situation where he has to act like an adult and simply tell you that he doesn't want to.

Saying something nice about someone's shoes—a microaggression, too? It appears that making a positive comment about someone's wardrobe is akin to belittling all of her life accomplishments. How dare you pay her a simple compliment for her good taste in clothing?

These are the ideas being taught at what we used to call institutions of higher learning. I've said dozens of times in previous pages that ideas always have consequences; they always bear fruit. Good ideas lead to good culture, good colleges, and good community; bad ideas lead to the opposite. Mature ideas lead to maturity, and childish ideas lead to immaturity. Wise ideas lead to wisdom, and foolish ideas lead to insanity. Ridiculous ideas result in ridiculous thinking, which leads to ridiculous behavior. Garbage in, garbage out. Ideological carcinogens lead to intellectual cancer. And the thing about most diseases is that they rarely stop with the individual. They quickly spread. It's called contagion. And today's society is sick with the disease of perpetual adolescence.

The thought police have every area of American life in their crosshairs. One of the American customs that has risen to the top of the "you-cannot-say-that" list is saying "Merry Christmas."

You read that correctly—Christmas. You can't say "Merry Christmas."

Christmas has been celebrated in the Western world since the fourth century. It has been a national holiday in America since 1870. It is a day as well as an entire season that has been tightly woven into the fabric of our nation and our individual lives. It drives much of our family cohesion and even dominates our nation's economy. But in spite of that, department stores and coffee shops have now declared the words "Merry Christmas" to be "triggering."

Target has the dubious distinction of being one of the first stores to go woke and purge the words "Merry Christmas" from its employees' approved vocabulary. Restricting festive greetings to "Happy Holidays," it seems, doesn't run the risk of offending anyone (except Christians), so it's clearly the acceptable benchmark for controlled thought and expression. Starbucks has joined in the progressive parade of condemning the two-thousand-year-old tradition of celebrating peace on earth and goodwill to men as a microaggression. "Happy Holidays" will not trigger anyone except those dastardly believers in the historical meaning of holy days. So let's empower Scrooge and speak nothing but humbug upon Saint Nicholas and his example of joy, self-sacrifice, and giving.

Is the Christian concern over progressive Christmas bigotry much ado about nothing? There is reason to believe that some of our cultural elites think so. According to John Boiler, the chief executive of an ad agency that produces marketing campaigns for major Fortune 500 companies, the reason to exclude Christmas from the marketplace is inclusion. No, your eyes didn't just cross. Yes, the smart folks who are running the multimillion-dollar market campaigns for our nation's biggest companies actually believe that the reason to *exclude* Christmas is "inclusion."

It's all simple economics, says Boiler. In the *Chicago Tribune*, he elaborates, "To say that you're only going to recognize one segment of your audience to the exclusion of others is not only bad socially and culturally, it is bad economically."[1] He goes further down this rabbit hole of self-contradiction: excluding Christians who believe in saying "Merry Christmas" is actually "the choice that is more inclusive—if you're also into making the most for your shareholders."[2] So to summarize: exclude people in the name of inclusion. Offend people in the name of being inoffensive. And de-recognize Christmas in the name of recognizing everything and everyone else. Makes sense, doesn't it?

In his book *The War on Christmas*, John Gibson notes a speech by CNN's Aaron Brown. Brown tried to deny there was a war on Christmas and argued that no one was worrying about Christ being taken out of Christmas. In response to the speech and the current movement, Gibson wrote, "It's no longer permissible to wish anyone a Merry Christmas. That's too exclusive, too insensitive. What if they're not a Christian? What if they're an atheist?"[3] Apparently these brilliant thinkers like Aaron Brown and his fellow movers and shakers at CNN have never stopped to think to ask the question: What if they are Christian? What if they feel excluded? What if they think you're insensitive? Haven't you just told these people that in the name of tolerance you will not tolerate them?

So, in order to include everyone, you are going to exclude Christ?

In order not to offend others with the word "Christmas"—a term accepted by just about all of Western civilization up until, oh let's say, the last five minutes—we unilaterally decided to remove Christ's name from a holy day that was specifically established to honor Christ. Forget this Christmas stuff and forget Christians. Let's just force everyone to say something innocuous like "Happy Holidays."

Do these people even know what the phrases "Merry Christmas" and "Happy Holidays" mean? Do they have any idea what the definition of their approved words truly is? Careful before you answer. The facts may surprise you.

Inclusive?

I have said it over and over, and I will say it again: words mean something. They have definitions, and definitions matter. As Aristotle chided, "How many a dispute could have been deflated into a single paragraph if the disputants had dared to define their terms." If we don't understand our words, their meaning can be manipulated, and we often end up arguing for things that may be the exact opposite of our words' original intent.

Such is the case with those who have pushed so aggressively to replace "Merry Christmas" with "Happy Holidays." They say that a "Happy Holidays" greeting includes everyone, is less religious, and is more acceptable in the current multicultural climate in which we live. But a closer examination of this example of PC policing reveals the lack of knowledge driving such an agenda.

In other words, the thought police are clueless. Look at the word "holiday." What does it mean? It might seem obvious. The word "holiday" is the combination of two words: "holy" and "day."

The argument of those attempting to secularize the Christmas season by calling it a holy day is obviously absurd. "Holy" is a religious word and means something that is sacred and set apart for God. Anything holy is something that must be preserved and kept whole. Something that is holy is sanctified, righteous, and pure. If something is holy it means that it is uncompromised and worthy of respect.

The second part of the word "holiday" is the word "day." Day refers to a twenty-four-hour period of time. Day is the acknowledgement of past, present, and future; the awareness of the clock; knowing that minutes and hours are passing and that ultimately they are God's to give and to take; that human beings have no say about the longevity or brevity of their lives.

Such an understanding of the brevity of life is found whenever we look at the Bible. James wrote: "What is your life? You are a mist that appears for a little while and then vanishes."[4]

A Jewish psalm writer penned these words: "Show me, Lord, my life's end and the number of my days; let me know how fleeting my life is. You have made my days a mere handbreadth; the span of my years is as nothing before you. Everyone is but a breath, even those who seem secure."[5]

Day is a term of self-limitation: the understanding that our days are numbered. Yesterday's memories. Today's responsibilities. Tomorrow's dreams. Made in the image of God, we stand alone in our awareness of time and of the divine dictate that "this is the day the Lord has made." We alone out of all God's creatures are obligated to keep it holy.

Do you see how the wisdom of those who wish to take Christ out of Christmas is flawed by their choice of using "Happy Holidays"?

Isn't it ironic that the "wise" who wish to secularize our culture actually do so by demanding we abandon "religious words" like Christmas, while at the same time arguing in favor of an even more religious word like "holiday"?

They want to believe in nothing, for a belief in nothing means that they become everything. Believing in no judge means that you are the only judge. Because there is no God they act like they are God. The only holy day is the one that excludes Christ and elevates them to the status of the word made flesh dwelling among us.

Can't these cultural gods who want to tell us what to think and what to say see that they are actually the poster children for a new religion? Can they not see that in their ill-informed efforts to remove a sacred day from our calendar they're actually using language that is even more sacred?

Something to Believe In

In 1990, the rock band Poison released what would become one of their signature songs, "Something to Believe In." The song was a call for something positive, something of substance. In the face of desperation and sorrow, the band called out for something to believe in. Throughout America and in other nations, the song was an anthem sung by masses of adoring fans frustrated with reality as they saw it around them. The song resonated with many in the early nineties as it spoke of the tangible emptiness of a life devoid of purpose. It was an anthem that rose above feelings of disillusionment, sorrow, suffering, pain, and injustice. It struck a chord.

We all need something to believe in—something more than just ourselves. A person without God is a person who believes he is God. The vacuum is always filled. Kill the God and you will fill the void with yourself as God. No human being can live without meaning, purpose, and definition. If there is no God, you will always create one. The problem is that we make for very poor gods. To quote Chesterton again: "Of all the horrible religions, the most horrible is the worship of the god within."

Inside the heart and soul of every man and woman is a desire to believe in something. Pascal called it a "God-shaped vacuum." But here's the thing about vacuums: it's a basic principle of physics that they are always filled.

We will either fill this void by our own choices and decisions, or someone else will fill it for us. There is no such thing as moral or ideological neutrality. Nothing is perpetually neutral. All vacuums are filled.

Though the high priests of postmodernity scoff at the thought of something beyond the here and now, the material and the temporal, you have the ability to think for yourself. You should never accept anyone's telling you what ideas are acceptable and what words you have to use and not use. You can choose what you do and you can choose what you say. Choose to believe.

Here is the beauty of maturity: human beings have freedom. We can think independently without being force-fed someone else's viewpoint. We can believe or we can disbelieve. It's a matter of choice. You can believe in freedom or you can believe in control. You can believe that God is God, or you can believe that you are God. You can believe in objective purpose and meaning, or you can believe nothing has purpose and meaning.

Jesus told his disciples how to find purpose, meaning, and peace. He said, "Do not let your hearts be troubled. You believe in God; believe also in me."[6]

There is a peace that comes from believing in something. In his last days before the crucifixion, Christ prepared his followers for what would come by reminding them that what they believed in would help them endure the crisis. His reminder is summarized in his basic question: "Who do you say that I am?" In other words, "What do you believe in?" Or yet another way to ask the question is, "Do you believe in Christmas?"

Christmas brings us back to the place where we are reminded of the hope of every generation, of peace on earth and goodwill toward men, of joy to the world, of the silent night, the holy night, the First Noel.

When you say "Merry Christmas," you are not simply expressing a pleasantry but rather expressing a worldview. By saying "Merry Christmas," you are reflecting a belief system that is central to who you are.

Over two thousand years ago the world was suffering through a cold, dark winter. Civil unrest was rampant in the Middle East, and the power of Western civilization was crumbling under the weight of moral decadence. Rome wielded the sword. Israel picked up stones. Fear killed freedom. Terrorism defeated trust. Even in the midst of the calm of Pax Romana there seemed to be a cloud of impending doom.

Today, as you watch CNN or Fox or read the paper, you may feel the same chill in your bones. The times are as disturbingly dark as a long winter's night. You may feel fearful. You may shiver as you try to shelter yourself from the freezing winds of nightly news. It's always winter but never Christmas, with one scandal and catastrophe after another taking the headlines.

But in the face of such cold winds, perhaps we would do well to remember the news of long ago when light shone on the hills of Bethlehem and a new song was sung. "Do not be afraid," the angel declared in a booming and confident voice, "for behold, I bring you good tidings of great joy." And on that night, winter began to melt away, Christmas sprang alive in a stable under the stars, and the human race was challenged to *believe* in Bethlehem.

Believe that the Bible is true and not transient. That it is inspired, not constructed. That it is accurate, not relative. That it is not to be added to nor subtracted from. That it is to be hidden in your heart and proclaimed with your mouth. That it is given by inspiration and breathed by God himself. That it is the inerrant, infallible, and authoritative written word of God that guides us in all matters of faith, learning, and living. That it need not be adapted to the desires of man but should be used by man to be transformed more into the image of God.

Believe in practicing wisdom. Too often, our actions fail to match our words. We would see our glaring hypocrisy on display if only we took time to examine ourselves. Be men and women of integrity. Work out your faith with fear and trembling, not as though you have already attained perfect faith. If you love him, you will obey him. What good is it if you call him Lord and do not do what he says? Show me your faith without deeds and I will show you mine by what I do. Remember the words of Dietrich Bonhoeffer: "Only he who believes is obedient, and only he who is obedient believes."[7]

Believe in Truth: the Logos, the Tao, the natural law, the revelation of God. Understand that there are *self-evident* truths that no human being can deny. Believe that such truths are revealed by God and not constructed by man, that they are objective and attainable, immutable and constant. Believe that truth gives salvation to the damned and freedom to the slave. Be energized by the unapologetic pursuit of truth. Wherever it leads, be confident in the words, "You shall know the truth and the truth shall set you free." Freedom is the antithesis of slavery. Slavery is the unavoidable outcome of lies, lies about who we are as people and lies about what is right and what is wrong. It is the result of lies about man and lies about God. Rather than being a victim swept up by the relativism of the day, believe in a truth that is absolute.

Believe in Christmas! It is Christ's Mass! Not Buddha's Mass. Not Mohammed's Mass. Not Hare Krishna's Mass. It's not Pelosi's Mass, Obama's Mass, your Mass, or my Mass. It is Christ's Mass! We can commercialize it, homogenize it, politicize it, and compromise it, but the bottom line is this: the word means something! It means you can believe in the primacy of Jesus Christ and that he is the beginning and the end, the way, the truth, and the life, the great I AM, the Word become flesh, Emmanuel—God with us—your Savior and your King, your Lord and your God, the Lion of Judah and the Lamb of God, your redeemer, your guide, your peace, your joy, your comfort, your life, your light! Believe that he is risen and incarnate: the Son of God, the alpha and omega, the lens of all learning, and the Lord of our daily lives. Believe that he is who he said he is in the seven "I am" statements in the Gospel of John—the light of the world, the good shepherd, the door, the resurrection and the life, the bread of life, the true vine.

Believe in the primacy of Jesus Christ.

Believe in the priority of scripture.

Believe in the pursuit of truth.

Believe in the practice of wisdom!

Believe what the Song of Songs tells us: "See! the winter is past; the rains are over and gone. Flowers appear on the earth; the season of singing has come."[8]

Believe in Christmas!

Believe in God, because you are not God!

Joy to the world, the Lord has come.

Merry Christmas! Long live the true King!

Stay in the Pen

"It is difficult to free fools from the chains they revere."

—Voltaire

Deceptive Freedom

Freedom can be deceiving. Or maybe better said, the appearance of freedom can be deceiving.

When you drive through the countryside and see a beautiful horse feeding on a ranch surrounded with fencing, does it seem free? When you walk through a neighborhood and hear a dog barking on the other side of the privacy fence, does it seem free? When you pass a school during recess and children are playing within the fenced-in playground, are they free? When you see that toddler playing with blocks in his playpen, is he free? When you look down at your wedding ring or see one on someone else, does it signal freedom?

All these examples suggest the opposite of freedom to many people. All of these examples are of animals or people who are confined in one way or another. All of these examples, at least at first blush, seem to be anecdotes where options are limited and someone or something is *stuck* inside.

The nearby nature preserve seems to offer more freedom for the horse than a fenced-in pasture. An open yard appears to give a dog more liberty than a yard that is fenced. It is the same with the enclosed playground for children, the playpen that restricts the infant, and the wedding ring that narrows the playing field down to one and one alone.

However, true freedom is often different from how it appears. If someone asked you who the one person was who most influenced the values and ideals of the American way of life—of freedom and justice—what would you say? Bruce Feiler tells us in his book *America's Prophet* that the answer is indisputably Moses.

A bit surprising, right? Even within Christian and Jewish circles, we don't realize how much Moses has been utilized to impact our understanding of freedom. To prove just how much of an influence Moses has had on our constitutional republic and our corresponding assumptions of what it means to be a free people, here's just some of what is a whole book full of evidence:

The Pilgrims claimed the inspiration of Moses as they fled the "Pharaoh" of King James in pursuit of their "promised land" in the New World.

George Washington spoke of the "Deity" who "delivered the Hebrews from their Egyptian oppressors" as being the same God who established the United States and watered it with "dews of Heaven" as it grew in independence and freedom.

The Liberty Bell is famous not for its excellent craftsmanship or its resonant sound but for the words of Moses inscribed on it: "Proclaim Liberty throughout all the land unto all the inhabitants thereof."

Columbus compared himself to Moses when he set out to cross the sea in 1492.

George Whitefield quoted Moses as he led the nation to salvation in the Great Awakening.

Thomas Paine compared King George to Pharaoh, Moses's nemesis, in his book *Common Sense*.

Benjamin Franklin, Thomas Jefferson, and John Adams all wanted Moses on the official seal of the United States.

Harriet Tubman adopted Moses's name on the Underground Railroad.

Abraham Lincoln was eulogized as Moses's incarnation at his funeral.

Franklin Roosevelt and Lyndon Johnson both drew upon the inspiration of Moses during wartime.

And Martin Luther King Jr. likened himself to Moses the very night before he was killed.

In 1973, political scientists Donald Lutz and Charles Hyneman decided they would do a comprehensive survey of "American rhetoric" during the founding era of our country. To this end, they took on the enormous task of reading everything published in America between the years of 1760 and 1807. The effort took them ten years and covered fifteen thousand documents. The goal was to settle the long dispute over what ideas most influenced the American Revolution. Was it the ideas of Enlightenment thinkers such as Montesquieu, Locke, Hume, and Hobbes? Or was it the influence of the ancient classics written by Plutarch and Cicero that most inspired our Constitution and our culture?

Well, the first sentence of their conclusion makes it quite clear: "If we ask what book was more frequently cited by Americans during the founding era," they said, "the answer...is: the Book of Deuteronomy."

And who is the author of Deuteronomy? Moses!

Feiler argues that Moses's influence on America is due to our founding fathers' understanding of this basic truth: only by trusting in the paradox of liberty and law can we ever hope to find the protection of our unalienable rights of life, liberty, and the pursuit of happiness and thereby be a free people and a free country.

The lesson we learn from Moses and the Exodus of his people from the bondage and slavery of Egypt is simple: freedom trusts in principles rather than power, people, or politics. Freedom honors the debate because it knows there's an answer, a true north, a measuring rod outside those things being measured.

Moses is synonymous with the law. And the Exodus is a story of freedom.

Like the fences that keep a horse in a pasture, the law is often thought of as the opposite of freedom. Even within scripture, law and liberty sometimes seem to be on opposing sides. But could it be that it only "seems" this way?

On closer inspection, none of the Old or New Testament authors ever suggest that God's laws restrict human freedom. The prophets, for example, never wrote that the law restricted freedom. Instead, they warned that disobeying God's law always resulted in brokenness, bondage, and the loss of freedom. In the New Testament, we read over and over again that we are "free in Christ." We are told that we "shall know the truth and the truth shall set us free." We are shown the paradox of discipline and freedom, liberty and law, in very clear terms when Jesus says that it is only those who give up their lives who will gain them.

The promise of the New Covenant, shared by the Old Testament prophets, was that God's people would be given a new heart and that their heart's desire would then be to love God, believe his truths, and follow his ways—in other words, to be set free by honoring God and his law.

There is a repeated paradox in scripture that frankly can't be missed if you bother to read it. God's law is always liberating, but the consequences of not living within the boundaries of God's law always compromise liberty.

In Deuteronomy, blessings are promised for keeping the law, and curses for not obeying it. Within the law, God's people found more liberty rather than less. When God's people kept his law, they enjoyed more freedom as opposed to more slavery.

If Moses has had such a profound positive influence on our national character and personal freedom, then wouldn't we want to consider his teaching and the lessons of history before departing from those laws?

G. K. Chesterton apparently agreed when he told us that if you get rid of the big laws of God, you don't get liberty, but rather thousands upon thousands of little laws that rush in to fill the vacuum. In other words, if we refuse to live by ten simple laws given to us by God (and frankly, Jesus seems have summarized them in just two!), we get reams upon reams of little laws imposed on us by the government and arrogant oligarchs in places like Washington, D.C., and San Francisco. These thousands of little laws are made up by the powerful and the privileged, the "smarter-than-thous" who think they know better than we do about how we should live, down to the point where they are now telling us which pronouns to use and how we should use the bathroom. This is absurd. This is not liberty. This is not freedom. It is fascism, pure and simple.

In ancient Rome, a fasces was a bundle of sticks, bound together so tightly that it couldn't be broken. You've seen it in some of the statuary in our national monuments. Go to the Supreme Court and look at the relief above the justices. In concrete and stone, you will see a fasces. It often has a hatchet head attached to it. The fasces represents the bond and strength of commonality, and it's where that we get the word fascism.

Fascism, as a form of authoritarian government, argues that you must be one of "us." You must be part of the collective. You must agree with us. You must think like we think. You must believe as we believe. You must act like we act. You must be one of us, or we will crush you. Submit or be expelled. Disagree and you are verboten. If you don't think like us, you're unwelcome.

This is what you see in the contemporary academy and beyond. Look at Brown and Berkeley and the University of Wyoming and Emory. Look at the stories that you see in the nightly news.

As you likely know, Berkeley fancies itself as the birthplace of the free speech movement. This is its unofficial motto. But today all you see is the exact opposite of free speech. Just turn on the nightly news: you will quickly see Berkeley students and faculty who do not believe in free speech or academic freedom at all. You will see protests seeking to control ideas rather than debate them. You will not see an open and robust exchange of differing points of view. You will see hundreds of students screaming that they feel offended and unsafe simply because someone dared to tell them they might be wrong. You won't see classrooms of curious students pursuing truth, but rather auditoriums full of crying picketers protesting anyone who believes in truth. The fact of the matter is that on many campuses, from Berkeley to Brown and everywhere in between, the rulers of the ivory tower have discarded truth in favor of tyranny. Power has replaced principle. Vengeance and violence have supplanted virtue. As David Horowitz has said in his book *Left Illusions*, the rule of the gang has replaced the rule of what is true and beautiful and good.

But perhaps the people who thought that the free speech movement started at Berkley were wrong all along. Berkeley is not the birthplace of free speech—Bethlehem is.

Just as ignoring Moses and his ten simple laws leads to less freedom rather than more, even more so will ignoring the one who said, "You shall know the truth and the truth shall set you free" lead to fascism rather than freedom.

In our attempt to be "free" we've broken down the moral and spiritual fences that defined and protected that freedom in the first place. We thought we'd find intellectual liberty by discarding the teachings of Moses and Jesus, but instead we've let the wolves of ideological fascism in and they are having us for lunch.

The Lesson of Blue

Contrary to popular thought, freedom is always found within fences. It's never found in tearing them down. Liberty is found within the walls of the law, not in the open fields or on the crashing shores of licentiousness.

Any talk of freedom versus fences makes me think of a 1970s ballad by Lobo:

Me and you and a dog named Boo
Travelin' and a livin' off the land.

Me and you and a dog named Boo
How I love being a free man.

When I think of that song I'm taken back to simpler times—times of AM/FM radios, summer camp, teenage friends, a dog's loyalty, "me and you and a dog named Boo." I also think of higher ideals, of the joy that comes from adventure, of the majesty of creation, of life and liberty, of "travelin' and livin' off the land."

But most of all, I think of humming that tune in the back of my mind as I watched my sons tussle and play fetch with their dog, Blue.

You see, Blue taught me something very interesting about freedom. Freedom is not free. True freedom always comes with a fence. If you have ever owned dogs, you know of their natural love for the outdoors, for hunting, for retrieving, and for a good run. You can almost see the laugh in a Labrador's eyes when she sees you are about to let her off her leash, when she knows she is about to romp in the fields or swim in a lake or roam in the local woods until exhausted. She absolutely loves freedom.

But you also know something else about dogs: they cannot be let loose from the restrictions of a chain, the confines of a kennel, or the boundaries of a backyard until they have first acquired discipline.

A dog can never enjoy "freedom" until she learns to obey. Oh, your dog may be "free" to ignore you and your commands. She may be "free" to walk away rather than sit, stay, heel, or come. She may be "free" to defy any rules or restrictions you try to impose on her. She may be "free" to think she is the master and you're not. But that would be a story filled with sadness, because you know that in her ignorant and stubborn way of living your dog is not experiencing a fraction of the freedom that could be hers. You know that if she would just listen, if she would simply accept some boundaries, if she would just obey your commands, that you could and would let her go. She wouldn't even need a fence or a tether anymore if you could trust her to stay out of the road and away from traffic. She could have total freedom and the run of the property if she would obey some basic rules established for her own good.

The simplicity of a dog's life—the lesson of Blue—has shown me over and over again that obedience is the price of freedom. No one ever experiences the "gain" of emancipation without first submitting to the "pain" of correction. Good things always cost something. We must remember that the payment for liberty is always found in the currency of submission. This is a lesson reinforced every time I see Blue run in the fields without a leash, free to respond to her master's voice alone.

Every athlete knows this is true. A soccer player knows he will never be free to play the game unless she disciplines herself to go to practice, listen to the coach, memorize the plays, and go through the daily grind of conditioning her body in preparation for competition. A basketball player knows he will never leave the bench unless he learns to do what he is told and play within the rules of the sport. Every athlete knows he or she has to honor the referee and respect authority. Anyone who thinks otherwise is merely an armchair quarterback who sits in his recliner on Sunday afternoons criticizing the real athletes. In athletics, freedom is the by-product of living within the boundaries. It is the result of setting oneself aside for the good of others. Freedom comes from learning to live within the rules, and discipline is a precondition to participation.

The same is true for musicians. If you don't learn the rules of music— of rhyme and rhythm and cadence—if you don't go to practice, obey your instructor, and discipline yourself to work daily at mastering your chosen instrument, the sound you hear will be not a concerto but chaos. Music comes to us through the beauty of rules, not in spite of them. There is no such thing as an undisciplined concert pianist.

Throughout his career, Martin Luther King Jr. stressed that liberation alone was not the singular destination for blacks. He believed that any free people must first understand and embrace the fundamental principles of human dignity, personal discipline, and self-respect. "As we struggle for freedom in America," he said, "there is a danger that we will misinterpret freedom. We usually think of freedom from something, but freedom is also to something. It is not only breaking loose from evil forces, but it is reaching up for a higher force. Freedom from evil is slavery to goodness." "Slavery to goodness," he insisted, comes with certain duties—"to respect others, to respect yourself, not to strike back, and to practice non-violence." Freedom, in other words, comes with responsibility. Liberation with self-restraint. Exodus with Sinai. The twin messages of America's founding—revolution paired with constitution— are the watchwords of America's founding and refounding.[1]

I began this chapter by sharing that freedom can be deceptive. What appears not to be free often is free, while what appears to be free is often enslaved. The horse was free because it learned to live within the fences of the pasture. He didn't have to be confined to a tether, a stall, or a corral. My dog gained more freedom when she learned where the boundaries of the property were and disciplined herself to live within them. It was then, and only then, that I let her off the leash and out of the pen.

Personal discipline is always a predicate to individual freedom. What appears to be restriction is really the opposite. It's the paradox of discipline and freedom, liberty and law.

There is always motivation to jump the fence, but freedom is found inside rather than outside the boundaries.

If you want freedom, build a fence.

If you want liberty, stay in the pen.

Wear the White Hat

"The smallest act of kindness is worth more than the grandest intention."

—Oscar Wilde

Old Westerns

In the early history of Western movies, and until more recent times, directors often put the hero in the white hat and the bad guy in a black hat. This contrast marked a stark distinction between the good protagonist and the evil antagonist.

There was a clear separation between good and evil. Young boys wanted to be the cowboy in the white hat. Girls swooned over him. His values were our values. He was the ideal man. He was the textbook definition of what it meant to be a "hero." He was the example of "how the West was won." Many a household was an extension of his attributes, his character, his values, and his integrity. Or at the very least, that's what they aspired towards. Though not every movie held tight to this formula, it was the norm from the 1940s through the 1960s. Things changed in the late '60s and early '70s. Like washing a brand-new red shirt in a load full of whites and ending up with an entire wardrobe that's pink, the white hats began to fade into gray. The lines blurred—not just in the movies, but in our neighborhoods and our homes as well.

Now, I understand that the old-time Western is more an ideal than a reality. I know Ozzie and Harriet were more of a cultural symbol than descriptions of real-life people. I understand that the squeaky-clean hero is an archetype and that the Lone Ranger is more a dream of what could be than a portrayal of what in fact is.

But isn't that what good art is supposed to do? Shouldn't literature inspire us to be better? Shouldn't movies tug on our souls and prompt us to reach for what could be, rather than to settle for what is? As our friend C. S. Lewis said, why be too easily satisfied in the muddy back alleys when we could be at the beach?

Today, in everything from Westerns to comic books and superhero movies, the antihero has become the main man. The clean-cut moral exemplars have been revised. There are tons of examples, but just consider the latest dark, gritty takes on superheroes such as Batman, the Green Arrow, and even Superman. Batman's evil nemesis, the Joker, now has a feature film all his own.

I'm not trying to be a movie critic here, but is it possible that this trend of spending so much time highlighting the imperfections of the human soul and even its darkest side is bearing some attendant consequences? Are our movies a symptom of a culture shift from celebrating good to fixating on bad? Are we too easily satisfied with sin when we've been promised the possibility of a savior? Are white-hat heroes no longer in vogue because we'd actually prefer to be entertained by vice instead of virtue? Finally, are we getting what we deserve—the dirt and grime of the back alley—because we mock the idea of beaches and oceans even being real? Is doing good no longer considered a good thing?

One area of disarray in our nation is the church. Author John S. Dickerson writes about the troubling condition of the American church in his book *The Great Evangelical Recession: 6 Factors That Will Crash the American Church . . . and How to Prepare*. Dickerson's key premise is that the church in America is dying. The evidence he presents to support this terminal diagnosis is multifaceted.

According to Mr. Dickerson, orthodox belief, church attendance, and denominational loyalty are all dropping precipitously. By way of attrition, a transition from the religious homogeneity of the baby boomers to the therapeutic deism of the millennial generation has led the church to flounder, flail, and lose influence in culture.

Political division and partisan disagreement will hasten the church's diminishing voice. There will be intramural splits. Church attendance will plummet. More than 2.6 million of those who are presently eighteen to twenty-nine years of age are predicted to leave the sanctuary and abandon biblical faith and traditional values over the next ten years. That trend will accelerate in the decades to come.

The number of nonreligious and secular Americans will skyrocket while the percentage of conservative Christians—that is, those who actually believe the Bible and seek to live their lives by its precepts—will decline to less than 7 percent of the American population in just a handful of years.

The days of a Christian majority are over, suggests Mr. Dickerson. The Judeo-Christian ethic is a thing of the past. But even more sobering than the rise of religious indifference and theological syncretism, he warns, will be the increase in animosity and outright antagonism toward biblical values.

The evidence for Mr. Dickerson's predictions is replete. Postmodernity's intolerance for and even hatred of orthodox Christianity is the stuff of the nightly news. Consider just a sampling of recent headlines:

A California pastor is arrested for reading his Bible in public.

A group of Catholic nuns is prosecuted for refusing to provide abortion-inducing drugs to its sisters.

The American Psychological Association considers amending its own *Diagnostic and Statistical Manual* to include a diagnosis called "intolerant personality disorder" as a description of any Christian who believes sexual behavior should be reserved exclusively for heterosexual marriage.

The European Union has passed a resolution declaring that all people who have an "aversion" to unbiblical sexual behavior are guilty of a "crime" equal to "racism, xenophobia, anti-Semitism, and sexism" and should be subject to "criminal penalties."

And just a few months ago, a British court ruled that a belief in Genesis 1:27 [the view that humans are created as distinctly male and female] "is incompatible with human dignity." The court went on to say, "In so far as those beliefs form part of [a] wider faith, such faith does not satisfy the requirement of being worthy of respect in a democratic society."

The list of grievances against Christians today seems endless. One could fill books with anecdotes calling for the church to be "thrown out and trampled underfoot" by those who hate its piety. Christianity, it appears, is now dysfunctional rather than desirable. Biblical values should be prosecuted rather than promoted. Followers of Christ are an insult to human dignity. Instead of deserving respect, we need treatment. We deserve to be punished.

In the face of such news, what are we to do? In this mess of anti-religious bigotry, what can we do? Do we take our ball and go home, or do we stay and fight?

There is an answer, and it is found in the message of the first-century church, a church that faced many of the same cultural challenges that we face today.

Our responsibility is quite simple and clear: do good.

In the midst of storms that had an eerie resemblance to some of the same dark clouds we now see on our own cultural horizon, Paul told the early Christians in Rome to "not repay evil for evil but to do good!"

He told the first believers in Galatia to "do good."

He told those being persecuted in Jerusalem to "do good."

He told Timothy to "do good."

Time and time again, the early church was admonished not to repay insult for insult, but instead to heed the very words of Christ and "do good."

Jesus couldn't have been clearer: "Let your light so shine before men, that they may see your good deeds and glorify your Father who is in heaven."

By responding to intolerance not in kind but rather by doing good, the church changed the world. Orphans were adopted. Widows were loved. The sick were cured. The poor were fed. The dying were saved. Women were honored. Children were wanted. Hospitals, schools, and colleges were founded. Slaves were freed.

Chesterton once said, "Christianity has died many times and risen again; for it had a God who knew the way out of the grave." The church's way out of what appears to be its present "grave" of cultural irrelevance is to follow that risen God who promised that the gates of hell would not prevail against us. With confidence in that promise, we are to "bless those who persecute us, bless and curse not"—and do good.

In the midst of plague, contagion, drought and disease, war and famine, dust bowls and stock market crashes, Christians kept doing good, and the world changed. In fact, historians tell us that these early Christians "turned the world upside down" and "set the world on fire."

The accomplishments of those early followers of Christ were truly astonishing, inspired as they were by their faith to do good in their communities. Saint Athanasius, whom many have called the author of the Nicene Creed, once wrote, "Seeing the exceeding wickedness of men, and how little by little they had increased it to an intolerable pitch against themselves... [Christ] took pity on our race, and had mercy on our infirmity." He went on to conclude: "Lest the creature should perish, and the Father's handiwork in men be spent for naught," God "took unto Himself a Body," a body that not only endures, lives, and breathes in his resurrection but also in his church.

Even those who openly place themselves somewhere along the atheist-agnostic continuum have to admit the redemptive power of the church. For example, Fox News contributor Greg Gutfeld, who describes himself as "non-religious," says, "I haven't been to church in years. But there is one thing I know: The church is a positive influence in communities, in terms of encouraging charity and neighborly concern." Likewise, Alain de Botton, author of *Religion for Atheists*, laments the loss of "discipline, structure, [and] community" in contemporary culture. He then goes on to come perilously close to affirming the Christian view of original sin when he says, "At heart [we are all] desperate, fragile, vulnerable, sinful creatures, a good deal less wise than we are knowledgeable, always on the verge of anxiety, tortured by our relationships, terrified of death—and most of all in need of God."

Then there is Matthew Parris, writer for the London *Times*, who extols the virtues of Christian missionary work in Africa: "As an atheist, I truly believe Africa needs God.… Removing Christian evangelism from the African equation may leave the continent at the mercy of a malign fusion of Nike, the witch doctor, the mobile phone, and the machete."

Indeed, the church is the salt and light of human history. It has preserved culture in the midst of disease, debauchery, and despair. It has been a beacon of hope in the darkest days of violence and oppression. The church has stemmed the tide of evil time and time again, even when the situation looked most bleak. Amid plague and contagion, it has been the apex of care and compassion. In times of terror and war, it has been God's "mercy on our infirmity" and His "pity on our race."

There is a simple secret behind the Allied powers' stopping the evil of Nazi Germany and Hirohito's Japan. The secret is that we believed our savior was God and not government. We elevated Christ, not conquest. We understood that we were the last best hope on earth for mankind. We understood the difference between good and evil. We were willing to fight to destroy one and defend the other.

Christians stopped the widespread practice of human sacrifice in polytheistic religions. Christians converted barbarians, evangelized the Vikings, and tamed the Wild West. Christians and the church have done good, a lot of good, even when they were surrounded by sin and perdition. Our world is better for it, and we should consider their achievements as an example for us all.

Jesus tells us—indeed, he promises us—that the "gates of hell will not prevail" against his church. Nothing can stop the "manifest power" of "a living God at work." He is not a "dead or static thing," but alive and well. Theologian Arthur W. Pink wrote, "Nothing in all the vast universe can come to pass otherwise than God has eternally purposed. Here is a foundation of faith. Here is a resting place for the intellect. Here is an anchor for the soul, both sure and steadfast. It is not blind fate, unbridled evil, man or Devil, but the Lord Almighty who is ruling the world, ruling it according to His own good pleasure and for His own eternal glory."

If we want to be truly different than the world around us, sometimes the best thing to do is to copy those who came before us. They were men and women of integrity who practiced what they preached. They didn't just believe it: they behaved it. They took up their cross and followed the one they claimed is God. If they could do it, you certainly can too!

And they did so by doing good.

Look at an Aerial Photo

"It would seem that not only is religion lacking in the schools—so is common sense."

—Ronald Reagan

Google Earth

When a hunter is scouting new places, an aerial photo (or what we used to call a map) can be one of his most important tools. The bird's-eye view shows the lay of the land: the topography, the rivers and streams, the hills, the roads, the paths. Any hiker, biker, hunter, or even tourist knows the importance of having a map. The map unifies what is otherwise a fragmented perspective, bringing everything together as a unified whole.

When you are down on the ground and without a map, you can only see what is immediately before you. You have no perspective. Your vision is limited to the next tree or turn in the path, the next fork in the road, the next building, the next rock and ridge. It's hard to understand proximity, place, and even purpose when you don't have perspective.

This loss of perspective, this myopic fragmentation of the way we see things, is more prevalent than ever in our current political discourse. With each new controversy, our loss of perspective regarding who we are as a free nation and free people becomes more and more pressing. We seem to see no further than the end of our nose. Segregation, victimization, and balkanization presently dominate the political stage and the public square. We're splintered rather than united. Democrats versus Republicans, liberals versus conservatives, young versus old, blacks versus whites, men versus women. The list of divisions, cliques, and groups seems endless. It's as if E *pluribus unum* has been flipped on its head. We now seem to be a nation built on the assumption of E *unum*, *pluribus*; dividing the one into the many.

Not only have we discarded common cause and common purpose, but we have also lost any modicum of common sense, rationality, logic, and civil discourse. When it comes to debate and a mutual exchange of ideas, it seems that we are content to crawl on our knees in the mud rather than get in a plane and fly.

If you listen carefully to any of the present political debates, or any of the current candidates' stump speeches, you will hear a litany of disjointed and contradictory ideas made by the same individual, the same party, and the same media pundits.

One politician says that he stands for children and government funding of infant care, while at the same time suggesting the government should be paying for the killing of these same children just seconds before they exit the birth canal and "officially" become infants.

Political candidates who pledge allegiance to one nation under God then act as if they are God.

In their oath of office they swear to "defend and protect the Constitution of the United States," but then they deny that our country has the right to establish and defend its own borders.

Like a hiker trying to navigate new property without a map, we fail to see the forest for the trees. Our perspective is limited. Our vision is truncated. We don't see the big picture. We are crawling on the ground when we could be using a drone. We need to get above the treetops to see the big picture.

Without a bird's-eye view, without a map, we can never make sense of the political landscape, nor any other landscape for that matter. No one even seems to be asking how these divisive positions and ideas can be unified into a cohesive and unified whole, a worldview that binds us together rather than tears us apart. Only then will we be able to return to sane political discourse and uplifting communal life.

Lacking a map for guidance, we've lost the foresight to successfully navigate challenging circumstances. We've become ultra-reactive, responding to individual events without any rationale or plan. Politicians and entire political parties rally behind a cause that represents the exact opposite of the values they championed just five minutes earlier. Political and moral attitudes change as quickly as you could flip a switch.

With the viral nature of social media, news and information travels faster and to more people than it has at any other point in history. Viewpoints change at an even faster rate. Our national temperament turns on a dime. Though large groups of Americans have been swayed in their political positions before, they've never done so at the speed of light.

We seem more and more willing to make rash decisions and rush ahead, never considering how our ideas, conclusions, and consequent actions are interconnected with history, reason, experience, and revelation. We act like we are islands unto ourselves and ignore that fact that we actually live in a community of interconnected people, values, and virtues.

No one is looking ahead or looking at the big picture. We're only reacting, only looking at one tree at time—maybe not even a tree, but just the bark. We need to step back and see the whole forest.

Did your parents ever tell you when you ran off ahead on a hike to make sure and stay on the trail? Why did they say that? Because that trail had likely been mapped out, and if you left the path who knows what might happen. You could step off a cliff.

Is it possible we would be much better off if, instead of running headlong into reactive politics, we pumped the brakes just a little and looked at the map? Maybe it wouldn't be such a bad idea to pause and look at the picture on the box before we assume we know how to navigate through the wilderness we find ourselves in.

One of the most remarkable aspects of our Constitution is how forward-thinking our founding fathers were. They anticipated not only issues of their day, but also how a certain set of ideas would impact the nation at large. They understood Locke and Montesquieu. They read Hume and Voltaire. They discussed Plato, Cicero, and Socrates. They knew their Bibles like the backs of their hands. They knew what Moses said, as well as Jesus. They could see backward as well as ahead. They knew where they had been and where they were going. They saw the promise of a republic and the dangers of a Robespierre. They understood the freedom of a covenant and the bondage of hierarchy. They saw the risks in the rule of the gang and the power in submitting to the reign of God. They believed in a big God rather than Big Brother. They had perspective. They saw not only the forest for the trees but also the paths and roadways that history and providence had carved on their behalf. They had a map and they used it. And who could possibly argue that we aren't better off today because of it?

We Have Issues

If there was any remaining question that corporate oligarchs and today's educational ruling class have near-Orwellian control over all of American culture, the aforementioned stories should remove all doubt. They are just a handful of countless examples of the contradictory buffoonery imbibed by the mainstream media and the ideological left. These stories are Exhibit A of how ill-conceived, poorly constructed, politically driven ideologies are literally stealing our First Amendment rights and subverting the very premise of our constitutional republic.

Take, for example, the story of Dr. Allan Josephson, a distinguished professor and former director of Child and Adolescent Psychiatry at the University of Louisville, who was recently not only removed from his leadership position but also informed that his contract for the 2019–2020 academic year would not be renewed.

His crime? Dr. Josephson dared to challenge the medical wisdom of "gender affirmation" and corresponding surgical sex-change treatments. In other words, for suggesting that it might not be all that great of an idea to tell a confused adolescent boy that he should cut off his penis. This man was declared verboten by Louisville's intellectual Third Reich and summarily fired.

Or let's consider the story of Hollywood star Mario Lopez, who, at the threat of excommunication, was forced by today's cabal of cultural high priests to bow in contrition at their rainbow altar and confess his sins. "What was his transgression?" you ask. Mr. Lopez dared to suggest that a three-year-old cannot be trusted to choose her own lunch, let alone choose her own gender.

For pointing out what 99.9 percent of all thinking human beings know to be obvious, the star of *Saved by the Bell*, *Dancing with the Stars*, and *Extra* was threatened with the loss of his career and therefore forced to issue a Cranmer-like recantation by day's end. One wonders if the Bloody Marys of the ivory tower and our nation's corporate boardrooms will demand his execution anyway.

Then, of course, there is the story of the New York City Queens Public Library increasing its budget and designating $25,000 of that increase to "Drag Queen Story Hours," shamelessly using children as young as four and five years of age as pawns in the dirty game of sexual politics.

Finally, who can forget the case of Marcia da Silva, owner of a home-based women's salon in Canada, who was sued by a transgender "woman" (otherwise known as a biological male, with all the accompanying physical accoutrements) because she (Ms. da Silva) refused to provide a Brazilian wax to this "woman's" scrotum. No, in case you haven't read this story, I am not making this one up.

And finally, even here in my hometown in the heartland, in the reddest of red states, Oklahoma—where we still believe that God is actually found in what you read in the Bible and not what you see in the mirror—corporate executives recently chose to champion a Pride Picnic in a local park, complete with rainbow flags and all things LGBTQ (which, by the way, makes them complicit in promoting everything I cite above).

Aside from the obvious arrogance of these cultural elites pushing these nihilistic values on all of American society, there is another common thread to these stories that is even more disturbing.

In case you missed it, here it is: today's ruling class has a palpable disregard for people and for what it means to be a human being. They are misogynists who deny that women are real, and they are proud of it. They are misandrists who deny that men should even exist because they are toxic.

When we step back and look at the proverbial aerial view of these colliding issues, we can see that women and girls are not winning. They are losing their privacy, dignity, and even their identity. And with regard to men and boys, how can anyone not see the psychological and physical losses being suffered by boys, who are being told as young as seven that they are not male but female, and who are being enslaved to a future of puberty-blocking hormones as well as chemical and even surgical castration?

In what world can anyone argue with a straight face that this is right? How can you possibly believe in the dignity of children while at the same time applauding as an eleven-year-old is paraded onstage in drag by a bunch of adults?

How can you possibly tell me you respect the value of a man when your default position on all that is wrong with the entire history of the world can be summed up in two words: "male toxicity"?

And how in the world can anyone claim to believe in the dignity of the human being when you kill more black babies in New York City each year by aborting them than you celebrate black babies by letting them be born?

Please just stop for a moment. Take a deep breath. Let the adrenaline subside. Stop fixating like a child on your individual, political, and emotional "trees" and take a grown-up look at the entire forest.

If our schools support women, then why do they teach our youngest girls that women are little more than leprechauns and unicorns, make-believe social constructs rather than biological facts?

If our politicians believe in women's rights, then why do they refuse to protect a woman's most basic rights?

If our progressive exemplars believe it's wrong for a man ever to force himself on a woman, then how is it ever right for these smarter-than-thou folks to force a woman to wax a man's genitals?

If you are so worried about the future of humanity because of global warming, then why do you support politicians who are telling you that human beings should be "reduced" by as much as 90 percent in order to save the planet from global warming?

Do you see this disconnect? As rational beings, we are smarter than this. But our national brain trust seems to be brain-dead. We will never be a people of common sense if we persist in doubling down on this nonsense.

If corporate executives truly believe in the dignity of women, then they should stop promoting the cultural appropriation by men of a status and identity they have no right to assume.

If "feminists" really believe in equal rights for the female, then they should stop pretending a female is a fantasy and a fabrication rather than a biological fact.

If our nation's leading universities really believe in gender inclusion, then why would they exclude a professor for defending the objective integrity of the female gender?

What could possibly be more degrading to a female employee than to have her employer publicly support the "blackfacing" of women in a manner that is just as cartoonish, grotesque, and insulting as it is when white people dressed up in literal blackface to mimic and mock people of color?

In his *Abolition of Man*, C. S. Lewis warned us of a time when we would become a characterless culture of "men without chests." But even the prophetic foresight of the Oxford don fell short on this score. Even Lewis didn't foresee the next domino to fall—that we would become a culture of "women without breasts," so proud that we have abolished man that we now proudly celebrate the abolition of women.

Perhaps if we would read a bit and reflect rather than simply react—if we would slow down, step back, respect each other, and have a civil, informed conversation—maybe, just maybe, this lunacy could be avoided and the outcome would be different.

As a former university president who made his entire career in the academy and its ivory tower, I believe in education. There is great value in the liberal arts and in studying the ideas of freedom, those ideas that have been proven throughout the course of history to liberate. But, as America's blue-collar voice Mike Rowe has rightfully said, the current educational model is broken. "We're just disconnected," says Rowe. "We're rewarding behavior we should be discouraging. We're lending money we don't have to kids who are never going to be able to pay it back to train them for jobs that don't exist anymore. That's nuts."[1]

In other words, a woke education is a joke education. We are bankrupting the next generation with student loans for degrees that are destructive of heart, mind, body, and soul. We are producing graduates who can't get a job and who can't even tell you a female is a fact. That's not only nuts, it's a sign of a people who are lost in the forest without a map.

Was It Helpful or Hurtful?

"To forgive is to set a prisoner free and discover that the prisoner was you."

—Lewis B. Smedes

Self-Destruction

What you're doing—is it helping you or destroying you?

For the most part, we blindly assume that whatever we're doing is helping us. No one wants to admit that our choices of attitude and action can be akin to intentionally choosing to destroy ourselves. There is a word for this phenomenon—it's called denial.

We rationalize and justify our actions. We give reasons and excuses. We tell ourselves and others that what we do is not a big deal. We have it under control.

We even convince ourselves that harmful behavior is actually helpful.

That lie we told? Well, it preserved a relationship.

That stuff we're smoking? Well, it's medicinal.

That drink? Well, it opened doors for a business deal.

Addiction? No way.

DUI? You're crazy.

Deception? Well, it made us all feel better.

We tell ourselves that none of this hurts us, but have we stopped to weigh the cost of those decisions?

Sometimes what seems helpful to us at the time is really nothing more than the thinly veiled, incremental destruction of our soul. Bitterness, anger, and unforgiveness fall into that category.

A Decade of Wasted Years

A pastor friend once shared a story with me. The story was a personal one he'd lived and one from which he had learned a valuable lesson. Unfortunately, more than a decade passed before he realized it and addressed the problem.

As a teenager, his father had left his mother for another woman. He never knew all the details, but from his vantage point, he knew all he needed to know. As a young man, he harbored bitterness towards the woman who became his stepmother, holding tight to his anger for nearly thirteen years. Every time he was around her, every time he saw her, he let her know how he felt. He was angry. He was bitter. He showed his disdain for her at every turn.

He was helping himself by not allowing himself to be a victim. So he thought.

If her name came up in a conversation, he made sure everyone knew his thoughts about her. These conversations always ended rather abruptly. He pulled no punches. He hated her and would never forgive her. He blamed her for hurting him, and he felt that his unforgiveness towards her was justified and even "helpful closure." Years later he came to understand the damage he was causing to his own heart, mind, and soul.

For thirteen years he held onto his rage and left a trail of broken relationships in his wake. Friendships were made and eventually shattered. Dating relationships were destined to implode. The only question was how long they would last before collapsing under the heavy weight of his righteous indignation.

In his late twenties, he came to the point of taking an honest look at himself. What he saw didn't look healthy. In fact, it looked sick and diseased. Something was wrong. His anger and resentment affected every area of his life. An emotional cancer was consuming every organ of his body, but first and foremost his heart, mind, and soul. Something had him shackled, and until those chains were broken his life would continue to unravel.

One afternoon, in the summer of 2005, he drove to his father's house, the house he had grown up in, to confront the woman he had hated for so long.

He took a step forward, one that he had once sworn he would never take. "I forgive you," he told her.

A short discussion followed, and he returned to his home two hours away. The burden that had weighed him down for so long no longer had power over him. As he drove, he looked in the rearview mirror, backward to a decade that had been wasted, and he didn't like the person he saw. When he considered his old self, he saw the haggard and disfigured face of resentment and indignation. But then he turned from the rearview mirror to the mirror on his visor. And looking straight into the present rather than at the past, he saw not that old face of revenge but a new face, a youthful face of repentance and renewal. His face now reflected hope rather than hate. He was a new creation. He had been born again.

A new day had dawned. Letting go of the past, offering forgiveness, and starting fresh affected his own life more than it affected his stepmother's life. He was set free from the shackles of his own terrible decisions.

Six weeks later, the pastor met his wife. They've been married for over a decade.

Would the story be the same if he had chosen to hold on to the bitterness? We cannot know the answer, but he would tell you that he would still be miserable if he hadn't forgiven his stepmother and moved forward in his life rather than remaining frozen in the past.

Following that night in 2005, he was alive again. For years, he had hurt no one but himself with his anger and resentment. How much of our lives have been wasted holding on to a grudge for something that happened years ago? What opportunities have been lost because we failed to forgive?

You might be saying, "Just because I haven't forgiven someone doesn't mean I am doing anything bad to them. I don't even say anything bad to them or about them. I just avoid them and try not to say too much when their name comes up."

Well, it sounds like your normal way of dealing with hurt is to avoid it, deny it is there, and go on with life. Even in the best of situations, this solution is anything but a mature or effective way to deal with the issue. Why? Because with a lack of forgiveness, you harbor anger towards someone who has wronged you, but you take it out on others who have done nothing to you.

Don't believe it? Try this and see what happens.

How many times have you experienced a rough day at work? Perhaps your boss criticized you for something you did not do. Maybe the project that was going along just fine for a year fell through, and from your vantage point, all you had done, all the work and effort, was for nothing. Perhaps there was a customer who just couldn't be pleased, and no matter what you did for him, he wasn't happy.

All of these are possible scenarios for any given day. Going to work is a venture into the great unknown because much of our work is at the mercy of others whom we cannot control and we cannot change.

Now, here is where the problem comes in. Do we take our frustration out on our boss, on those who cancelled our project, or on the unreasonable client? Do we discuss the issue at work and leave the job, the disappointment, and the results of the issue at the office before we go home?

Most of us tend to do the opposite. We have a bad day at work, go home, and take it out on our family and friends. The children find that our temper is short and endure our frustrated dismissal of their questions. The kids grow louder, and the irritation which we thought was small and controllable turns into a blaze of indignation that threatens to consume everything in sight. Your spouse becomes the victim of your silence and your condescension. Even though you "didn't say anything bad about people or to them," those who didn't have anything to do with the situation receive the fallout because of the way you transferred your frustration to others.

The same rule holds true with unforgiveness, resentment, and bitterness. Those closest to you who have nothing to do with the original situation are the ones who receive the brunt of what your lack of forgiveness bottles up inside.

"Well, you don't know what they did to me. If they did that to you, you wouldn't forgive them either," you might retort. You might be right on that. I don't know what they did to you. But what I do know is that you and I don't play by the same rules we impose on others.

You and I are very quick to condemn others for holding grudges, but when we do the exact same thing, we are oh-so-slow in holding ourselves to the same standard. It becomes "do as I say, not as I do." The rules are for thee but not for me.

Do you see the hypocrisy here?

You expect something that you are not willing to give. Being an adult requires forgiving others because you know you need it as much, if not more, than anyone else. A lack of forgiveness will stunt your growth. Angry people are immature people. Anger will keep you locked in a moment that happened a year earlier, five years earlier, or in the case of that pastor who hated his stepmother, thirteen years earlier. You don't grow. You don't mature. You are frozen in time.

"Well, I would never do what they did."

Really? Are you sure?

Once there was a man who was sentenced to death for crimes he did not commit. As he was marched through the street to his execution, he was beaten and mocked. He was slapped, spit upon, and sadistically executed for the sins he never committed.

Who spit on him? Who mocked him? Who killed him? You and I did. Your selfishness put Jesus to death just as if you were the Roman soldier swinging the hammer or thrusting the spear. My sin makes me as guilty as Pilate and the Pharisees. How are my lies and power trips any better than theirs?

Our attitude and actions led to the death of a righteous man.

Do you need forgiveness? I sure hope you aren't arrogant enough to suggest you don't. We all need forgiveness. Without forgiveness, we are damned to live miserable lives now and for eternity.

When we ask for forgiveness, we expect to receive it, don't we? I will bet that you once apologized to someone expecting that person to give you immediate forgiveness so you could continue on with your life without the guilt you had hanging over your head. Shouldn't you hold yourself to the same standard that you expect from others?

Jesus explained why being a forgiving person is necessary if you also expect to be forgiven. He said, "For if you forgive other people when they sin against you, your heavenly Father will also forgive you. But if you do not forgive others their sins, your Father will not forgive your sins."[1]

You expect to be forgiven. The expectation is that you, in turn, will forgive.

Many churches over the past few decades have failed to teach this basic truth of Christ's Gospel and human psychology. Forgiveness is an action, not just a prayer. Forgiveness is a priority—a first thing—and the secondary things of life will never be had until we learn to forgive unconditionally. Unforgiving people are unforgiven people. And such people are like the woman C. S. Lewis describes in *The Great Divorce* who had grumbled for so long that she actually became little more than a perpetual grumble:

> The question is whether she is a grumbler, or only a grumble.
> If there is a real woman—even the least trace of one—still
> there inside the grumbling, it can be brought to life again. If
> there's one wee spark under all those ashes, we'll blow it till
> the whole pile is red and clear. But if there's nothing but ashes
> we'll not go on blowing them in our own eyes forever. They
> must be swept up...

The whole difficulty of understanding Hell is that...it begins with a grumbling mood, and yourself still distinct from it: perhaps criticizing it. And yourself, in a dark hour, may will that mood, embrace it. Ye can repent and come out of it again. But there may come a day when you can do that no longer. Then there will be no you left to criticize the mood, nor even to enjoy it, but just the grumble itself going on forever like a machine.

People who need grace should be people who extend grace. Otherwise we become people who know nothing of grace at all. And let's not forget that without knowing grace we are all damned. "For it is by grace that you're saved...it is not of yourselves, lest any man should boast."

Those who are desperate for mercy (and you and I surely are) should be merciful to others.

And those who feel like we deserve a second chance should be the first to grant a second, third, and fourth chance to someone else.

World-Changing

Nearly everyone dreams of changing the world in some way. Some have ambitions of helping starving children, building houses for the homeless, or rescuing animals that have been abused.

Making contributions such as these to our community drive many to believe that they are impacting and changing the world. Producing art and music are ways to make a mark and make a difference. We all want hope and change!

But though our plans are noble and lofty, we often fail to see the most basic and proven tool in all of human history that will—without fail—bring that change we so desire

To forgive others is to change the world.

We need look no further than a Texas courtroom to prove my point.

On October 2, 2019, Brandt Jean shook the political landscape, as well as our cultural assumptions of justice and jurisprudence. Brandt Jean was the younger brother of Botham Jean, a young man who was shot and killed by an off-duty police officer named Amber Guyger.

Tensions rose in the community with the initial charge of manslaughter. Eventually the charges were raised to murder. In the trial, Guyger was found guilty and sentenced to prison. That provided the moment for Brandt to make an impact on the world by doing what most people would never do.

In one of the most moving moments seen in an American courtroom in recent memory, the young man told the woman who had just been convicted of murdering his older brother that he forgave her.

Nothing could undo what had been done. Hating her and holding a grudge would not breathe life back into his brother. Carrying the anger with him throughout the rest of his life would cheat him more than it would punish her. When the moment came to speak, he was ready.

"I wasn't ever going to say this in front of my family or anyone," said Brandt Jean, "but I don't even want you to go to jail. I want the best for you because I know that's exactly what Botham would want. And the best would be to give your life to Christ. I'm not going to say anything else. I think giving your life to Christ would be the best thing that Botham would want you to do. Again, I love you as a person and I don't wish anything bad on you."

What a moment! Everyone expected Brandt to condemn and even demand the death of his brother's murderer. He had the right to hate. But instead he chose to forgive and offer hope. He wouldn't be the only one.

Echoing his younger son's remarks, Brandt's father responded, "I felt the same way. I wish I could've extended you the same courtesy. That is what Christ would want us to do...if you will not forgive, neither will your father forgive you. I don't want to see her rot in hell. I don't want to see her rot in prison. I hope this will change her life...."

Forgiveness erupted in a place of law and order. Two family members had taken Jesus at his word, turning the other cheek rather than striking back. The moment, however, was not over.

Presiding judge Tammy Kemp responded by stepping off the bench and handing Guyger her personal Bible. She said: "You haven't done so much that you can't be forgiven. You did something bad in one moment of time. What you do now matters." She then whispered in Guyger's ear, "Ma'am, it's not because I am good. It's because I believe in Christ. None of us are worthy."

This is the heart of the Gospel. None of us are worthy. None of us are good. All of us are sinners, and I am chief among them. We are all broken, and if we think we are justified, we stand condemned already.

The good news of the Gospel is that we can rise above resentment and revenge and become new creations in Christ. We don't have to let others control us. We don't have to be enslaved by perpetual victimization. We do not have to be held in bondage by the sins of others and the sins we find in ourselves.

We can forgive. We can be forgiven. We can be saved!

Saved from anger.

Saved from vengeance.

Saved from self-righteousness.

Saved from self.

Martin Luther said, "For still our ancient foe, doth seek to work us woe; His craft and power are great, and armed with cruel hate, on earth is not his equal."

John Newton cried, "There are two things I know: I am a great sinner, and Jesus is a great savior.... Amazing Grace, how sweet the sound that saved a wretch like me."

The cycle of "cruel hate" is broken only by grace: God's toward you, and yours towards others. And grace is made real only through the act of forgiveness.

But against this beautiful testimony of Brandt Jean, the ugly grudge of anger and resentment waited on the steps just outside the courtroom that day. Chants of "No justice, no peace" rang out. "How many of us does it take to get justice?" One pastor even shouted, "It's amazing how quickly injustice can be seized from the hands of justice. This is a travesty."

The sad thing is that Brandt Jean clearly understood something this pastor did not. The story of his brother was not one of recompense or payback. Botham's story was not about demanding justice. It was about granting forgiveness. Or, as Brandt so beautifully said, it's about "giving your life to Christ" because that "would be the best thing Botham would want you to do."

The actions of Brandt and his father, as well as the judge, should have silenced the cries of that angry mob and unforgiving pastor. What a juxtaposition of worldviews. A young man forgives and changes everything for the good. A preacher demands justice and changes nothing, not even himself.

The example Brandt, his father, and Judge Kemp set will ring throughout the halls of justice, not just in the courts of Texas but through all eternity. Brandt changed the world. Brandt changed heaven. He followed the example of Christ, one of forgiveness, one of doing to others what you would want done unto you, and the earth shook and the angels sang. This is true hope. This is true change.

Judge Kemp offered her closure to the story by saying to Brandt, "Thank you for the way you modeled Christ." But if you listen carefully, you might actually hear Jesus extending his perfect summary: "Well done, thou good and faithful servant. Well done."

The organization Freedom from Religion Foundation, upon hearing of the actions of Judge Kemp, began its attack. The organization claimed that Judge Kemp had proselytized in the courtroom, and in doing so had broken the law. What had been a beautiful moment of forgiveness became fodder for an organization that refuses to see that fogiveness is the only way the circle of victimization and vengeance can be broken. Freedom from Religion Foundation completely missed the point. Forgiveness is the only way to stop the hate that they claim to hate. While waving banners of "Love Is Love" and "Love Trumps Hate," this organization's recalcitrance proves over and over again that it would rather see people be held in the vicious cycle of victimization than see people freed through the forgiveness and grace of Christ.

You can be like the protestors, or that pastor on the steps of the courthouse, or even like the folks at Freedom from Religion Foundation. You can be someone who is completely controlled by his desire to get his pound of flesh, or you can choose to do what Brandt did: forgive and turn the other cheek.

Forgiveness breaks chains because forgiveness sets you free.

There Is No "I" in Team

"Individual commitment to a group effort—that is what makes a team work, a company work, a society work, a civilization work."

—Vince Lombardi

All about Me

The desire for celebrity status is pervasive. It's everywhere. For years, we have watched as the individual has become the focus of nearly every venue of life. The old athletic axiom, "There is no 'I' in team," has been traded for "Hey, look at me!"

This mentality has produced terrible consequences for our society. Rather than being members in a band of brothers, we have become warriors in solitude. There is no more obvious evidence of this than in higher education.

If you do not believe that there is a concerted effort to divide the nation, I have some oceanfront property in Nebraska I would like to sell to you today. The people responsible for this agenda push their message through cable news, newspapers, social media, and colleges and universities. They think that if they can get people to focus on themselves, their grievances, and their victimhood—that is, what divides them rather than what unifies them—the very fabric of the nation can be taken apart strand by strand. Or as Solomon told us, "A cord of three strands is not quickly broken," but a cord of one is defenseless. In other words, divide and conquer.

And this strategy is working. Just look at the divisive rhetoric of contemporary politics or the transparent "us-against-them" agendas, otherwise known as intersectionality and critical race theory, that are rampant on our campus greens from coast to coast.

Adults are acting like children, crying, "That's mine" and "You hurt my feelings." They are unashamed of throwing juvenile tantrums until someone gives in and strokes their little egos. They apparently do not even care that they are obviously being played like a banjo by those plucking the strings in Washington, Hollywood, and faculty lounges throughout the nation.

We see calls for segregation rather than integration. Those seeking to control us shamelessly work to divide us by race, gender, sexual orientation, voting tendencies, economic status, nationality, height, weight, educational level, religion, age, and whatever else can balkanize us into competing groups with irreconcilable demands.

In a 1975 interview, Ronald Reagan told Mike Wallace, "If fascism ever comes to America, it will come in the name of liberalism." This foresight of the "Great Communicator" has proven prescient. Indeed, ideological fascism has come to America, and it has come at the hand of progressives waving flags of safe spaces, mircoaggressions, trigger warnings, and victimization and vengeance on college campuses across the land. Under these flags you see "children" from the ages of eighteen to eighty throwing tantrums in the public square and demanding that we give them every plastic toy and piece of candy they want, or suffer the consequences of their wrath.

When your god is diversity, unity will not be tolerated. If our priority is diversity, a second thing, we will never realize the first thing of unity. Diversity is self-centered. At its core, it divides. It is grounded in the premise of me-against-you and us-against-them. It is childish. It is selfish. It says "give me mine." It is the antithesis of Christ's admonition to die to self.

Children are, by nature, individualistic and insular. They don't care about much other than themselves. They want what they want. Other people and their needs may never even cross their minds. Adults, to the contrary, have hopefully matured enough to understand that life isn't just about them. They see the wisdom of promoting unity rather than division, integration rather than segregation, us rather than me and mine, a United States rather than divided states. Adults ought to care more about a common cause of personal righteousness than the divisive demands of our personal rights.

Adults see the value of hundreds of hands working together, rather than one person's hands clapping in midair. What would a symphony be if there was only one person playing a triangle and no other musicians or instruments? Adults see that the full orchestra makes the music that inspires us to consider things grander than ourselves. Adults understand that inspiration comes from outside, not inside. You don't inspire yourself; something bigger and better and beyond you is always the source of your inspiration.

When we reverse the order and focus on second things, we get neither first nor second. It is only by dying to self—that is, setting aside our childish individualism—that any human being will ever find his true identity.

True identity isn't found in race or gender. It isn't found in personal grievances or our narcissistic infatuations. We are neither Jewish nor Greek, male nor female, slave nor free. We are human beings, and selfless unity rather than self-centered demands is the first thing.

Focusing on first things actually works. Evidence of this can be found in innumerable examples, from music to athletics, from government to marriage and family dynamics. But one seminal example is found in the Acts of the Apostles.

In the earliest days of the church, growth was explosive. Why? Luke wrote, "All the believers were together and had everything in common. They sold property and possessions to give to anyone who had need."[1] Christ was the focus of these first churches in Acts. The assembly included men and women, apostles and new converts. All these people were from various socioeconomic backgrounds, nationalities, races, and ethnic groups. There was clearly every potential for them to focus on their differences and what divided them. They could have started talking about diversity and multiculturalism. They could have started lecturing each other about critical race theory and intersectionality. They could have focused on how one group was privileged at the expense of another. But we hear none of that. Why?

It is simple and clear: the first church understood the first thing. The Body of Christ was more important than individual believers. Christ was more important than their individual complaints. Unity was more important than diversity. They sold what they had and gave it to others, not because they were socialists but because of their Savior. They didn't give of their wealth because they thought everyone deserved their fair share. They gave all they had because they knew that no one, themselves included, deserves anything! Bottom-line, they knew it wasn't about them.

Professors, politicians, pundits, and even preachers do our nation great harm by enabling young people to miss the first things by fixating on those that are second. As Richard Neuhaus warned, such ontological dyslexia only brings the "profound bigotry and anti-intellectualism and intolerance and illiberality of liberalism." This enabling of perpetual adolescence and its fixation on "me and mine" is growing with each decade. It is stunting the development and growth of our kids and our culture. We are force-feeding our progeny with a steady diet of individualism and diversity rather than the higher ideas of sacrifice and unity. Why are we surprised to see a generation of self-centered adults frozen in childish claims of entitlement and demands for "their fair share"? We have set up those who follow us for failure by encouraging them to believe that their safety is more important than their neighbor's soul. We have taught them that they are entitled to everything rather than obligated to give anything.

William Wilberforce suggested that this enabling of such misguided thinking is the antithesis of love. He said, "If you love someone who is ruining his or her life because of faulty thinking, and you don't do anything about it because you are afraid of what others might think, it would seem that rather than being loving, you are in fact being heartless."

The fixation on "faulty thinking," that is, on second things, brings cries of "microaggressions" and calls for "trigger warnings." It runs from the debate rather than toward it. It brings exclusion rather than inclusion, segregation rather than integration, and cries for comfort rather than accepting the challenges of confrontation. These deficiencies do not rectify themselves over time, but rather grow like a cancer with each passing year. The more the second things are highlighted, the less likely anyone will ever understand that they are not the first thing.

But instead of encouraging people to grow up and think, act, give, and serve like adults, our nation's brain trust thinks it's a good idea to bring in a herd of goats for our precious little snowflakes to pet so they can insulate themselves even further from any of the demands of life that might compromise their sense of self.

Talk about faulty thinking!

Over the past thirty years, I have had at least fifteen different college students live with my family. These students became part of our family while they attended college. The majority of these kids were from different cultures, and some were even from different countries.

In my house, unity, not diversity, has been our concern. We are family, pure and simple. We see character, not color, age, nationality, or social status. We celebrate what we have in common and don't worry about how we differ. We focus on the Savior and not the self. We hold each other accountable to righteousness and don't defend our rights. We are much more interested in what is good than what is safe.

My family's identity is in Christ, not in individual grievances. Everyone under my roof "is a man and a brother," nothing more and nothing less. There are no subdivisions. My home is a uni-versity, not a di-versity. It is a place where everyone is expected to act like an adult and not behave like a child. My home is not a day care. Our priority is to know and honor God, not to stand in line to pet goats.

Forget what the proponents of diversity are telling you. They say they are striving to bring unity to all people, but their goal is to create further division with each passing day. They say they champion what brings us together, but in actuality all they strive to do is highlight the very things that divide us. Playing on race, they create a greater separation between people of different colors. Calling for bipartisanship, they castigate and cast out those who hold different beliefs and values.

While claiming that they accept all people as they are, they reject those who do not conform. These progressives call for people to come together while finding pleasure in driving them further apart each day.

But the historical vision for America is, in fact, the opposite. It is a vision of uniting rather than dividing. Our history is one of a people of differing views who came together, unified, and with common purpose fought for human dignity and freedom. What our founders held in common was of far greater value than any of their differences. They understood the paradox that the more a government focuses on what the individual is owed, the more all individuals will be owned by that government.

Today, these foundational principles of freedom are clearly under attack by people who know very well that the way to more power is through more division. A cord of one strand can be broken. A cord of three cannot.

Why divide when the strength of numbers offers greater odds of success?

Why be satisfied with diversity when we can have unity?

Why pet goats when we could actually be serving God?

Strength is found in unity with one another and in the unity that we share in the Body of Christ. Knowing that we are the *imago Dei* leads us to see others as creations of God. The followers of Christ welcome and include everyone of all backgrounds and races in the common bond.

Adults see beyond the small differences. Every day, we associate with those who pull for different sports teams. We speak and fraternize with those who listen to different styles of music and prefer different kinds of food. We know that when we stop talking about diversity and celebrate unity we quickly forget about ourselves and can think almost exclusively about others.

Adolescents talk about their differences. They segregate. They divide. The irony, however, is that the second thing of the self is always self-defeating. If all you care about in life is getting your rights, your safe space, and your pound of flesh, if your focus is on little else besides your individuality and your identity, then you may get what you want in the end, but you may not like it.

If your focus is on you, then you'll get it and little else.

There is no "I" in team, and those who think there is always lose.

Sit at the Exit Door

"We are all faced with a series of great opportunities bril-
liantly disguised as impossible situations."

—Chuck Swindoll

True Adults

A society desperate for leaders always turns its eyes to the next generation, and there are lots of reasons to be searching for leadership now. With the rapid decline in original thought, intellectual freedom, and open debate, the masses fall in line; American education seems intent on producing propaganda rather than sound pedagogy. Teachers seem to yearn for carbon copies of themselves rather than graduates who can think for themselves. Today's academic establishment is in the business of requiring that students follow the leader and punishing those who dare to lead.

Leadership is out. Falling in line is in.

The maturity and confidence to think for oneself is, at its heart, a call to leadership. Adults obviously have more freedom than children. They've lived long enough to learn from their mistakes, discard the ideas that didn't work, and embrace the good ideas that have merit. True adults don't have to conform to arbitrary authority, for they can see the reasons underpinning justified authority. They lead as much as they follow, and they follow as much as they lead. They understand the paradox of discipline and freedom. They understand what it means to lead through example rather than by threats.

Real adults understand that leadership is service, not sanctimony. They intuitively take to heart the words of Christ: "He who loses his life will gain it.... The first will be last and the last will be first." Adults are willing and eager to stand alone, and by their integrity (and sometimes with very few words) to say "Follow me" when everyone else seems all too willing to follow the crowd.

Flight Time

On any plane, someone needs to sit at the exit door. If you've flown much you know that these seats are often desirable because they come with extra legroom. But during the preflight briefing from the flight attendant, those sitting in that row are always asked if they're willing and able to carry out the responsibilities of helping others get off the plane in case of an emergency.

I've flown my fair share, and I've yet to see anyone refuse to accept this leadership role. Everyone says, "Yes, if there's a crisis, I am willing to keep my head about me, step forward in the midst of panic, and do what no one else will do. I'll open the door and lead."

But, by and large, the exact opposite is true for our society as a whole. Few seem willing today to say, "I don't care what everyone else does or doesn't do, I will lead."

This hasn't always been the case.

Once a year, on September 11, images of the most horrific attack on the mainland United States flash across our television screens. We've all watched it over and over. We've all seen the planes as they crash into the towers, heard the frantic phone calls that were recorded, and watched the Twin Towers collapse to the ground as an immense cloud of dust and debris billows its way down the streets and alleyways of New York City.

However, if you aren't watching closely enough, you will fail to see the heart of leadership on display. In the midst of the chaos, firefighters, police, and paramedics ran towards the catastrophe, not away from it. Rather than preserving their own lives and their own safety, they instinctively did their duty. They weren't thinking of their own lives, but of the lives of everyone else. They're true leaders, true heroes. They didn't even seem to think about themselves at all. Sacrifice seemed as natural to them as breathing. They saw the reward of risking it all to save someone else.

This is leadership.

Leaders set convenience aside.

Leaders have conviction and a driving principle.

Leaders take the reins rather than waiting for others to do so, regardless of the cost.

The leaders that history judges as the greatest are those whose love for a cause and passion for a mission are so irresistible that they cannot help but take the reins, and others can't help but rally behind them. They cannot remain silent. Inaction isn't an option for them.

Leaders don't stick their finger up to determine which way the proverbial winds are blowing. They don't pander or reverse course because of polls or popularity. Leaders boldly declare with Martin Luther, "Here I stand, I can do no other."

Many of those who ran into the buildings on 9/11 lost their lives trying to save the lives of others, sacrificing all they had for those they did not know. They acted not for fame or for glory, not for selfish preservation or self-centered gain. They led simply because it was the right thing to do.

Another unforgettable story of the leadership witnessed on 9/11 came from the plane that crashed in a field in Shanksville, Pennsylvania. Realizing that the plane had been hijacked and believing that it would be used to cause more damage, passengers rose up to take down the hijackers. The phrase "Let's roll" grew in popularity after it was spoken by Todd Beamer as he and several of his fellow passengers made their way toward the hijackers.

The determination and courage of Beamer and the crew of Flight 93 will never be forgotten. Rather than sitting still and following instructions, they fought back. They gave their lives and, in turn, saved the lives of thousands who were the intended targets of a terrorist attack.

Learning How to Lead

For over seventeen years, I was blessed to be a university president. During my time at the helm, we went from financial exigency to a model of fiscal health. Enrollment more than doubled, as did revenue. Debt was paid down to zero, and net assets increased from about ten to forty million. Perhaps most important, the university's reputation grew from relative obscurity to one of national leadership. We were repeatedly cited as a champion of academic freedom and religious liberty.

While sailing a ship that even Peter Drucker once said was impossible to sail, I learned some key lessons, some through success, some through failure, all by God's grace and patience. Here are just ten lessons I learned while navigating some rough waters.

The first lesson in leadership is that if you inherit failure, break it and start over!

It's been said to "never let a good crisis go to waste." This is so true. If you're blessed to be given charge of a sinking ship, you can always lead more boldly than you could if you were given charge of an organization that was healthy. Take advantage of the opportunity presented to you—don't squander it. Rather than trying to cure cancer by applying a Band-Aid, cut out the disease. Get rid of the carcinogens. Break the cycle and don't hesitate to "break" the organization. This is the only way you will save it. Don't let the crisis go to waste; use the crisis as a launchpad for something different, a new plan to elevate the company to a new level.

The second lesson is this: if you inherit success, don't break it. If you're fortunate to take over something that is working, build upon the success. If your organization enjoyed success before you were hired, your job is "don't screw it up." Celebrate the things that have worked, and keep doing them. The person running the leg ahead of you in this race was likely there because he was faster. Be thankful that he gave you a lead in the race. Focus on the goal at hand and whatever you do, don't drop the baton. Take it and run forward. Your ego will tempt you to ignore all the good and give too much time and attention to the few things that are bad. Leaders are always tempted to throw the baby out with the bathwater, but true leadership identifies success and builds upon it.

The third lesson in leadership is that if you want to make everyone happy, don't be a leader. Choose something different. Go sell ice cream. If you're a friend to all and an enemy to none, then you're a leader of no one. The best coach I've ever had made it very clear that he was not my friend; he was my coach. He understood that in order to instill in me what I needed to learn, he could not try to appease me all the time. He needed to push me. He needed to test me. Rather than being my friend, he had to stoke the fire inside me to prevail. If popularity becomes more important to you than doing what's right for your organization, then it is time to resign and move on to something else. The pursuit of popularity is a waste of time.

A fourth lesson I learned was to never, ever bend a knee to the mob. When you are right, stand tall and refuse to bow. Paul wrote, "Therefore, my dear brothers and sisters, stand firm. Let nothing move you. Always give yourself fully to the work of the Lord, because you know that your labor in the Lord is not in vain."[1] It is better to lose your head than to lose your soul. Conviction is respected. Weakness is not.

The next lesson of leadership is that truth matters most. Demand truth. Defend it. Model it. Never compromise it. Never supplant it. Truth must always be first. Without truth, there is no trust. Without truth, you'll have no team. Devoid of truth, there is no change. If there is no truth, there is no Gospel and there is no grace. There's a reason that Jesus defines himself as the Truth. Truth is central in leadership; the minute you put something else ahead of truth is the minute you have designated yourself to be a follower, not a leader. Simply put, if anything is more important to you than truth, you have already failed.

Building upon that lesson of leadership, the next lesson is this—if you're not willing to lose the battle, you'll never win the war. Your personal success is not the top priority. Yes, there are a plethora of books on how to find success, maintain success, how to look successful, and so on, but true leadership is not about you. Be willing to suffer defeat for doing what you know is right. The cause for which you fight is more important than your resume or your career. Rather than turning and running away from the storm, which is the natural reaction of followers, run straight into the face of the storm. Wave the banner! If you win, great, that is God's grace. If you lose, who really cares? At least you went down fighting.

The seventh lesson in leadership is to care enough to confront others, because, after all, your job isn't to be liked. Those who talk about grace, love, and compassion in juxtaposition to truth, discipline, and confrontation are nearly always more interested in being liked than they are in leading. If you were to Google "enablement," you'd likely find their picture. Case in point—parents who strive to be liked by their children at the expense of discipline raise up kids who have no idea that there is a universe that they are not the center of. Children who are always liked by their parents are almost never liked by anyone else. Grace without truth, love without discipline, and compassion without confrontation are false dichotomies. You can't argue for water without rain, harvest without seed, or heat without fire. If you want to raise up a virtuous people, then you will have to confront their vices.

Too much support and too little challenge result in stagnation rather than growth. Remember the truth that "the Lord disciplines those he loves." If the Lord uses discipline to encourage growth, our leadership should do the same. James wrote, "As the body without the spirit is dead, so faith without deeds is dead."[2] The same can be said about leadership that is more concerned with likability than productivity. Being liked is far less valuable than being respected. Leaders choose to confront rather than enable.

The eighth leadership lesson I can share with you is to double down and refuse to give in to doubt. Everyone has his friends and foes. We all will be criticized by some and praised by others. The way to know who to listen to is simple. What is their track record? If your critics are failures in their own lives, ignore them. If the critic is someone who has nothing invested and chooses to sit on the sidelines and critique in the hopes of tearing you down, I suggest you take to heart the words of President Theodore Roosevelt: "It is not the critic who counts; not the man who points out how the strong man stumbles, or where the doer of deeds could have done them better. The credit belongs to the man who is actually in the arena, whose face is marred by dust and sweat and blood...who at worst, if he fails, at least fails daring greatly, so that his place shall never be with those cold and timid souls who neither know victory nor defeat." Roosevelt knew that leaders are more often torn apart by those who are not in the arena than by those who are.

If those who offer criticism are more successful than you, listen to them. If those challenging you have done more than you, then humble yourself and pay attention, for the words they share and the insight they offer may be what helps you to grow into a more effective leader. Be grateful for their coaching. If those complaining about you have never accomplished much, take their criticism with a grain of salt. When small men and malcontents are shooting arrows at your back, it's a sure sign you're going in the right direction. Keep going! Stay the course. Double down and refuse to give in to doubt.

The ninth lesson in leadership is to stay on message. Too often, the vision is lost when the message is vague or shifting. Staying on point is key to becoming effective as a leader. It has been said that the three secrets to success are repetition, repetition, and repetition. Winston Churchill famously modeled single-minded focus when he said, "Never give in, never, never, never, never...never give in." If there is anything that distinguishes great leaders from those who fail, it is the confidence to speak their message with clarity, confidence, and passion and to do it over and over and over again. Be a one-string banjo. Wave your banner and then wave it again and again. Shout your battle cry, then shout it over and over again. Sooner or later, you will find that not only do those following you believe it, but so do you! By staying on message, you model the consistency and the vision necessary to lead others.

The tenth lesson in leadership is if you want to find a snake, listen for the rattle. Some say that there are only two things that are sure in life: death and taxes. It is hard to argue with that truth. However, I would add a third surety in life: gossip. Leaders are maligned. Leaders are the targets of every form of innuendo, exaggerated stories, and even blatant lies. If you are leading, sure as the sunrise, people will gossip about you. The best advice I ever received was this: "Mr. President, just be quiet." When people speak ill of you, "just be quiet." When naysayers sow dissension about you, "just be quiet." When you're falsely accused, "just be quiet." The best way to find the snake is to listen for the rattle. Let the snakes around you make the noise and eventually they will be the ones to lose their heads. Don't rattle. Let your success do the talking. Just be quiet and lead!

But all of the guidance in the world is for naught if we're unwilling to put what we've learned into action.

James said, "Do not merely listen to the word, and so deceive yourselves. Do what it says."[3] Just as knowing what Jesus said is only as good as the commitment we make to apply those truths to our lives, the same can be said about leadership. Being taught how to lead is only as good as the application of those lessons in our lives.

Adults do things, children do not do. Adults lead, children follow. Adults take action, children sit. Adults run toward storms, children run and hide. Adults rush into falling buildings while children watch and wait to see what happens. Adults have courage, children cower.

Followers are content in being directed where to go, what to do, what to think, and how to feel. Leaders, however, set the tone. The tone doesn't set them. Their leadership begins at home; setting the example for the family extends beyond those walls and into the world, impacting their company, community, and church.

No one can force you to lead. Leading is a decision to sacrifice. It is a decision to serve. It is a decision to give rather than take, to run rather than stand, to fight rather than surrender. It is a decision to rush into a burning building. It is the commitment to wave the banner of "Let's roll," and having the confidence to know that if you lose waving that banner, it doesn't matter.

Leading is about conviction. Leading is about commitment. Leading is about courage and character. It's about acting like an adult rather than a child.

Conclusion

Still a Mess

I had a friend tell me that when he was a kid he and a buddy would fish in the irrigation reservoir of a rice field. To get to their fishing hole, they usually traveled the long way around through the woods. An old ATV trail wound around and took them right to the high banks of their fishing spot. But once, instead of taking that long path, they become impatient and took the short one.

The reservoir could be seen clear as day from the main road; it was on the other side of a rice field. My friend and his buddy didn't have much experience around rice fields. They took off, with tackle box and reel in hand and waterproof rubber boots on their feet.

It didn't take them long to begin sinking deep into the muddy field. It was like had quicksand. The mud was so thick and sticky that by the time they were halfway across they were involuntarily barefoot. In their tracks, each had left one boot, then another, a sock, and another. The field was a muddy mess. They had taken the wrong path. They had chosen the wrong road.

Robert Frost uses this imagery in his classic poem, "The Road Not Taken":

> Two roads diverged in the yellow wood,
> And sorry I could not travel both
> And be one traveler, long I stood
> And looked down one as far as I could
> To where it bent in the undergrowth...
> I shall be telling this with a sigh
> Somewhere ages and ages hence:
> Two roads diverged in a wood, and I—
> I took the one less traveled by,
> And that has made all the difference.

As I reflect on this classic poem, as well as on the story of my friend and the rice fields, I can't help remembering a recent conversation I had with a good friend.

It was one of those fun times where the hours flew by like minutes, where disagreement was serious and sincere, yet cordial and honest—where confidence was tempered with compassion, and where both parties likely shared the proverbial hope that "as iron sharpens iron, one man sharpens another."

We each held views—strong views—that were essentially opposite. I believed and expressed one idea with great conviction. He did too, but to different ends. He advocated one ideological course while I espoused another. We disagreed. This was the kind of wrestling that good education is made of.

In our debate, both my friend and I moved from one idea to another, sparring and jockeying for position. But in the end, all of our arguments basically came down to one key question: is the Truth real and, if so, how can we know it?

After too much time had elapsed, both of us realized that we had to move on to other things. My friend concluded by calling for a truce. He said, "I think there are many paths up the mountain, but the beauty is that they all lead to the summit. Perhaps we shouldn't argue so much about which road we choose, but agree that it isn't the specific path that's important, but rather the journey."

Now, on the surface, this argument seems quite attractive. Surely the path isn't nearly as important as the destination, is it? If we go to the left or to the right we will end up in the same place. Won't we? Clearly, the winding road is just as good as the straight one; the broad gate just as worthy as that which is narrow. And doesn't respect for tolerance and diversity require us to embrace all ideas, all values, all lifestyles, all worldviews, and all paths as essentially equal?

The Indian-born philosopher Ravi Zacharias, who argues for the knowable and singular nature of God's revelatory truth, addressed these same questions recently in a Q&A session of the Veritas Forum at Harvard University. After his presentation, Dr. Zacharias was confronted by a student who contended that all religions are the same, all lead to the same place, and all have equal theological, ontological, and epistemological veracity. There are many paths up the mountain.

Zacharias's response was pointed as he paraphrased the poet Stephen Turner: "[Indeed] all religions are the same except for their understanding about the character of God, of the cosmology and meaning of the universe, of human nature, of human value, of the nature of reality, of ethics, the good life, charity and kindness, sexuality, suffering, joy, hope, salvation, and our eternal destination of either heaven or hell."

Dr. Zacharias made his point crystal clear. Yes, indeed, all worldviews are the same, except in matters critical to life and death, social and physical health, as well as temporal and eternal existence. Hmm, I guess if you set these minor issues aside then all roads do lead to the same place.

Do we really believe that all paths lead to the same destination, or does common sense as well as basic logic tell us that if you want to get from point A to point B, it is wise to get a map and follow a guide? Maybe choosing to follow the one who shows the way, who knows the right path, and who exemplifies the right ideas will help us avoid getting lost.

As I conclude this book, I leave you with this simple admonition: perhaps we would all do well to consider the words of Robert Frost and remember, as we approach the diverging cultural roads before us, that choosing the one less traveled does make all the difference.

One road will lead to perpetual dependence mired in cultural and personal immaturity. The other road, while longer, more time-consuming, and, at times, even a bit of a nuisance, is one that may appear to be "less traveled by," but in reality the number of people who have chosen it is not nearly as relevant as the quality of people who have done so.

This road is one of rock, not sand. This is the high road that avoids the muck and mess of today's political swamp. This road is one with signs along the way that say, "Walking Is Better Than Crawling," "Plates Don't Have Legs," and "Don't Fall in the Pool." This is a path where others who are just a half-step ahead of you are willing to offer counsel, such as, "Pack Jumper Cables," "Don't Argue with the Mechanic," and "You Aren't Webster." These folks have learned from their own mistakes, and they might share a story or two with you about how it's important to "Brush Your Teeth before Leaving Home" and how fruitless it is to try to "Nail Jell-O to the Wall." This is the road where many who have gone before you have left notes advising you to "Bring Your Umbrella," "Listen for Omaha," "Be the All-Beef Patty," and don't forget to "Stay in the Pen." These are people who know to "Wear the White Hat" and "Look at an Aerial Photo." They know "There is No 'I' in Team," and they are willing to "Sit at the Exit Door" and lead.

Bottom line: this is the path for adults, not children. They have chosen the road less traveled. They have chosen wisely, and it has made all the difference.

Notes

Lesson 1: Walking Is Better Than Crawling

1. Jennifer Harper, "Gee, Thanks Mom and Dad: 35% of Millennials Still Live at Home," *Washington Times*, June 28, 2019, https://www.washingtontimes.com/news/2019/jun/28/35-of-millennials-still-live-at-home-survey-finds/.
2. "30% of Millennial Men Have No Job," MoneyTips, July 5, 2019, https://www.moneytips.com/30-percent-of-millennial-men-have-no-job/885.
3. Aimee Picchi, "How Marriage Became a Status Symbol for Millennials," CBS News, February 1, 2019, https://www.cbsnews.com/news/how-marriage-became-a-status-symbol-for-millennials/.
4. "30% of Millennial Men," MoneyTips.
5. Kelsey McShane, "After Millennials 'Killed' Chain Restaurants and Bras, Will This Controversial Piece of Bedding Be Next?" *USA Today*, March 27, 2018, https://www.usatoday.com/story/life/nation-now/2018/03/27/top-sheet-no-sheet-surprisingly-fierce-debate-uncovers-strong-opinions-bedding/461978002/.

Lesson 2: Plates Don't Have Legs

1. Robby Soave, "Colleges Cancelled Exams for Students Traumatized by Trump's Election," *Reason*, November 10, 2016, https://reason.com/2016/11/10/colleges-cancelled-exams-for-students-tr/.
2. Adam Dachis, "'Life Is 10% of What Happens to Me and 90% of How I React to It," Lifehacker, June 24, 2012, https://lifehacker.com/life-is-10-of-what-happens-to-me-and-90-of-how-i-rea-5873131.

3. 2 Thessalonians 3:10 (NIV).
4. Galatians 6:9 (NIV).
5. Jordan B. Peterson, *12 Rules for Life: An Antidote to Chaos* (Toronto: Random House Canada, 2018).

Lesson 3: Don't Fall in the Pool

1. U.S. Department of Transportation, "Traffic Safety Facts: Distracted Driving 2014," NHTSA, April 2016, https://crashstats.nhtsa.dot.gov/Api/Public/ViewPublication/812260.

Lesson 4: Pack Jumper Cables

1. Ecclesiastes 3:2–4, NIV.
2. Marcel Schwantes, "Science Says 92 Percent of People Don't Achieve Their Goals. Here's How the Other 8 Percent Do," Inc.com, July 26, 2016, https://www.inc.com/marcel-schwantes/science-says-92-percent-of-people-dont-achieve-goals-heres-how-the-other-8-perce.html.
3. Katharine Hepburn, *Me: Stories of My Life* (New York: Ballantine Books, 1991).
4. Matthew 7:24–25 (NIV).
5. Matthew 7:26–27 (NIV).
6. 2 Corinthians 4:8–9 (NIV).
7. Chuck Colson and Catherine Larson, "The Lost Art of Commitment," *Christianity Today*, August 4, 2010, https://www.christianitytoday.com/ct/2010/august/10.49.html.
8. Henry David Thoreau, *Walden* (New York: Thomas Y. Crowell & Company, 1910), 433.

Lesson 5: Don't Argue with the Mechanic

1. John McCormack, "Paul Ryan: The Biggest Problem in America Isn't Debt, It's Moral Relativism," *Washington Examiner*, November 18, 2011, https://www.washingtonexaminer.com/weekly-standard/paul-ryan-the-biggest-problem-in-america-isnt-debt-its-moral-relativism/.
2. Craig Vincent Mitchell, *Charts of Christian Ethics* (Grand Rapids, Michigan: Zondervan, 2006).

Lesson 7: Love Lost

1. 1 Corinthians 13:4–8 (NIV).
2. 1 John 4:8 (NIV).
3. David Jeremiah, *The Jeremiah Study Bible* (Nashville, Tennessee: Worthy Publishing, 2013), 1590.

Lesson 8: Brush Your Teeth before Leaving

1. Matthew 6:33 (NIV).

Lesson 9: Jell-O Doesn't Nail to the Wall

1. Goodreads, "G. K. Chesterton," Quotable Quote, https://www.goodreads.com/quotes/40380-impartiality-is-a-pompous-name-for-indifference-which-is-an.
2. Mike Thom, "'I Am Not a Christian': Joshua Harris Announces 'Deconstruction' of Faith," CHVNRadio, July 29, 2019, https://chvnradio.com/articles/i-am-not-a-christian-joshua-harris-announces-deconstruction-of-faith.
3. Galatians 1:10 (NIV).
4. "Public Trust in Government: 1958–2019," Pew Research Center, April 11, 2019, https://www.people-press.org/2019/04/11/public-trust-in-government-1958-2019/.
5. Joshua 24:14–15 (NIV).
6. 1 Corinthians 15:58 (NIV).
7. Franklin Graham, "We Must Not Remain Silent," *Decision Magazine*, March 1, 2019, https://billygraham.org/decision-magazine/march-2019/we-must-not-remain-silent/.

Lesson 12: Listen for Omaha

1. Brett Bodner, "Peyton Manning Explains the True Meaning of His 'Omaha' Call," *Daily News*, April 13, 2017, https://www.nydailynews.com/sports/football/peyton-manning-explains-omaha-call-article-1.3051914.
2. Proverbs 14:12 (NIV).
3. Christopher Gates, "Mike Tice to Retire from Coaching Because 'Players Don't Want to Be Coached,'" Daily Norseman, February 6, 2018, https://www.dailynorseman.com/2018/2/5/16977354/mike-tice-retire-from-coaching-players-dont-want-to-be-coached.
4. Peter Robinson, "Tear Down This Wall," *Prologue Magazine* 39, no. 2 (Summer 2007), https://www.archives.gov/publications/prologue/2007/summer/berlin.html.
5. Proverbs 24:16 (NIV).
6. Romans 12:2 (NIV).
7. "Transform," Dictionary.com, https://www.dictionary.com/browse/transformed.

Lesson 14: Wish Everyone a Merry Christmas

1. Julie Zauzmer, "'Merry Christmas' or 'Happy Holidays'? How National Chains and Mom-and-Pop Stores Choose," *Chicago Tribune*, December 23, 2016, https://www.chicagotribune.com/business/ct-chain-stores-merry-christmas-happy-holidays-20161223-story.html.

2. Ibid.
3. John Gibson, *The War on Christmas* (New York: Sentinel, 2005), xvii.
4. James 4:14 (NIV).
5. Psalm 39:4–5 (NIV).
6. John 14:1 (NIV).
7. Dietrich Bonhoeffer, *The Cost of Discipleship,* revised edition containing material not previously translated (New York: Macmillan, 1972).
8. Song of Songs 2:11–12 (NIV).

Lesson 15: Stay in the Pen

1. Bruce Feiler, *America's Prophet: Moses and the American Story* (New York: HarperCollins Publishers, 2009) 248–49.

Lesson 17: Look at an Aerial Photo

1. Joseph Curl, "Mike Rowe Rips Student-Loan Crisis: 'We're Rewarding Behavior We Should Be Discouraging,'" Daily Wire, November 9, 2019, https://www.dailywire.com/news/mike-rowe-rips-student-loan-crisis-were-rewarding-behavior-we-should-be-discouraging.

Lesson 18: Was It Helpful or Hurtful?

1. Matthew 6:14–15 (NIV).

Lesson 19: There Is No "I" in Team

1. Acts 2:44–45 (NIV).

Lesson 20: Sit at the Exit Door

1. 1 Corinthians 15:58 (NIV).
2. James 2:26 (NIV).
3. James 1:22 (NIV).

Index